# WINE HIKING
# SWITZERLAND

## EXPLORE THE LANDSCAPE OF SWISS WINES

# WINE HIKING
# SWITZERLAND

## EXPLORE THE LANDSCAPE OF SWISS WINES

ELLEN WALLACE

HEL·· VETiQ

For Nick, Liam and Tara,
who have each, in different ways,
helped me see that you can find happiness
on alternative paths.

# TABLE OF CONTENTS

# 1

## INTRODUCTION

# ABOUT ELLEN

Ellen's first "slow travel" ventures on foot and bicycle began as a student in Wisconsin, USA, where she also worked in a restaurant with a sommelier who taught her that wine was a world to explore, not a beverage. Her later geographic travels have taken her, slowly, across China in 1985 on a bike, around the British Isles and much of Europe by bike or on foot, across Cuba and parts of Africa. Switzerland remains her favourite place for walking. Her wine travels have taken her through even more cultures with their history, literature, languages, agriculture, and art. She ranks Switzerland's artisanal wineries as among the best in the world today. The nature of their vineyards and the work of the vignerons is closely intertwined with the mountains, lakes, rivers and forests that Swiss hikers love. This is what artisanal terroir wine means.

Her advice: take the time to listen to wines, to learn about them and not just drink them, and you'll discover that the places you hike are part of their story. Even if you are not a wine-drinker you can still appreciate the centuries-old stories whispered to us by vineyards.

Ellen is a widely published news, travel and wine journalist who today writes novels, essays and books, including *Vineglorious! Switzerland's Wondrous World of Wines*, an introduction to Swiss wine.

# ABOUT THE BOOK

Put one foot in front of the other and you'll go somewhere. Add a good map and a plan and you'll land somewhere interesting. Wine follows the same pattern: try one wine, then another, and you'll find wines you like. Add a good hike where there are vineyards and a visit to an artisanal winery and wine becomes far more interesting.

I've been writing about Swiss and other wines for decades, but I gradually realized I'm preaching to the converted: people who read about wine are mostly professionals or wine geeks. In 2019 I decided to find a way to help people enjoy wine without giving them more information than they need. I stopped writing wine notes and put my blog on hold. I decided to find ways to focus on the places and people and plants and animals that come together to produce something beautiful that friends can share.

At just the right moment Helvetiq asked me to create a series of Swiss hikes which would give people of all ages a nice day out that would end with a good, hand-crafted glass of wine for the adults. One hike, one wine, one winery. I loved the concept, based on the successful Helvetiq *Beer Hiking* series. I could interest people who like wine in going to new places and learning new things. Wine is an essential thread in the Swiss cultural fabric, just as hiking is. Slowly, one foot forward and one wine tasted at a time, readers would increase their knowledge about Swiss wine and thus their pleasure in it.

The selection for each hike began with the wine and winery so that the book could present wines from several grape varieties, in several styles, from all of the Swiss wine regions. There are six official Swiss wine regions but since one is German-speaking Switzerland, which covers far more territory than the others, I've created sub-sections of East and West based on an arbitrary "center" line but also geographic similarities that affect their wines. Some wineries are large, some just one person, but all are artisanal, focused on making terroir wines. The highest vines in the country are at about 1,100 metres above sea level, in Vispertermi-nen in Valais – and these are exceptional. Elsewhere, vines rarely grow above 900 metres a.s.l.

Once the wine and winery were selected I began to create the hikes, always starting and ending with public transport and using hiking trails that are part of the well-maintained Swiss trails system for as much of the route as possible. Most are cross-country, some are along the edges of rivers or lakes. A handful take hikers through cities for part of the trail.

Lace up those boots and get moving – and "Cheers!" from me when you sit down for that fine glass of wine.

# 2

# HERE'S HOW IT WORKS!

# CHOOSE THE WINE OR THE HIKE

NAME OF THE HIKE ———→

REGION ——————

LEVEL OF DIFFICULTY ——→

MAP ————————→

NAME OF GRAPE(S)
NAME OF THE WINE

INFORMATION
ABOUT THE WINE

INFORMATION
ABOUT THE HIKE

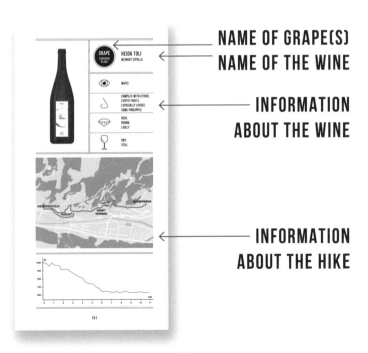

# LEVEL OF DIFFICULTY

The classification is determined by the most difficult parts of the hike. Sections that are particularly difficult are mentioned in the description of the itinerary. The level of difficulty is based on good weather conditions. Poor weather, snow or ice can increase the difficulty and have an impact on the time.

## EASY

The footpaths are wide and the slope has a slight incline. If they are not muddy due to long periods of rain or snow, you can even push an all-terrain stroller. Signs and markings are yellow.

## MODERATE

The hiking trails are paths that are clearly visible with little risk of falling. You can wear lightweight walking shoes. Dangerous sections are secured by a railing. Walkways or bridges cross the streams. The signs and markings are yellow.

## DIFFICULT

These are mainly mountain trails with steep and narrow sections and difficult terrain. Certain areas can present a risk of falling. You might need to use your hands in order to keep your balance.

Your feet might get wet crossing streams. These hikes require sturdy shoes with skid-proof soles. It's necessary to be surefooted, not to be afraid of heights, and to know mountain dangers (weather, risk of slipping, falling rocks). Signposts and markings are white-red-white.

**Note**
A few of the trails are marked MODERATE/DIFFICULT when most of the hike is moderate, but there are small difficult sections where hikers will see white-red-white markings.

# BEFORE SETTING OFF

## CHECK YOUR GEAR

# WEATHER

Detailed weather forecasts are available at:
www.meteoswiss.admin.ch

# MAPS AND ORIENTATION

The maps shown in this guide should be seen as guidelines only. We recommend that you always have a map with you:

- Paper map:
  The Swisstopo map reference that corresponds is provided for each hike. The sheets refer to the official "Swiss hiking" maps that you can buy on the internet:
  https://www.swisstopo.admin.ch.
  Look for Paper Maps on the menu or by searching. These are continually being improved, and a fairly recent addition to the standard 1:50,000 Hiking Maps is waterproof 1:33,333 Hiking Maps. The larger size makes it easier to read many details.

- Smartphone map: for each hike the GPX hiking files can be downloaded from www.helvetiq.com. To access the tracks you will need to have a mobile application that lets you open GPX files, of which there are several. I used Swisstopo, the official mapping service, to plan hikes, and edited them for clarity using the SwitzerlandMobility (network for non-motorized traffic) app. Place and road names are based on official SwissTopo versions, or in the rare cases when not provided, Google Maps names.

# HOW TO GET TO THE STARTING POINT

All the hikes are easily reachable by public transport. For times and itineraries: www.sbb.ch (English available).

# PATH CONDITIONS AND SNOW

The network of hiking trails is created and maintained by associations of volunteers. There is no official service that provides information about current trail conditions, but local tourism offices are often able to help.

The WSL Institute for Snow and Avalanche Research provides detailed maps and information on snow conditions: www.slf.ch (English available).

# USEFUL PLANNING LINKS, SOURCES

Swisstopo (www.swisstopo.ch) and SwitzerlandMobility (www.schweiz-mobil.ch/en) provide recommended hiking trails and tools for planning. The latter has details for all national, regional and local hikes and several special hikes. The online versions are slightly different from the apps; both are useful and free of ads, unlike some of the private mapping apps.

Swisstopo's 3D modeling is often useful, but should be used with some caution.

SwitzerlandMobility offers "Plus" for an annual fee that allows you to access hikes even when a signal is not available as well as to save, edit and share your hikes. Note that the online version is available in German, French and Italian but not English, while the app is available in English.

For a primer in GPX files, if you're new to online mapping:
https://hikingguy.com/how-to-hike/what-is-a-gpx-file/

Swiss Rando and cantonal Rando groups have a wealth of hiking information and shared hikes. https://www.schweizer-wanderwege.ch/de/home (German, French, Italian)

A variety of useful addresses can be found on the private site, www.wandersite.ch.

# DOGS

Dogs are welcome on most hiking trails in Switzerland, but they must be on a leash in nature parks, reserves, many local parks and in particular if there are cows nearby. Most of the hikes in this book require dogs to be leashed some of the time.

# WINERIES

**Important note: be sure to contact the winery you want to visit in advance, and try to be as precise as possible about your arrival time.** Artisanal wineries are small operations, sometimes with just one or two people, and they rarely have regular opening hours. All are closed on Sundays and even those with regular hours are usually closed Saturday afternoons. The reason is simple: they spend an enormous amount of time working in the vineyards and then again in the cellar, and they sell mainly to restaurants and distributors. Occasional visitors are not their primary source of money or best way to market their wines. That said, to a one they will give you a warm welcome because they care about sharing their wines with people who will take the time to learn.

To help you find the wines in the area if the winery is closed, I've listed a couple of restaurants or cafés or wine bars (and sometimes shops) as alternatives. Please note that post-Covid the ownership and offers of many restaurants are in flux and I apologize if the wine mentioned here is no longer available.

# INTERESTING FACTS

## PRODUCTION & GRAPES

A STANDARD BOTTLE IS
**75 CL**

PINOT NOIR
**28%**

CHASSELAS
**26%**

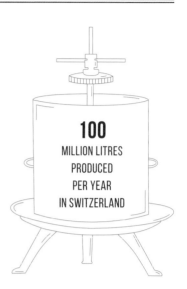

**100**
MILLION LITRES
PRODUCED
PER YEAR
IN SWITZERLAND

MORE RED THAN WHITE PRODUCED BY ALL REGIONS EXCEPT VAUD

## CONSUMPTION

SWISS PEOPLE ARE THE
**4TH**
LARGEST CONSUMERS
OF WINE WORLDWIDE

PER CAPITA
**33**
LITRES/YEAR

1.3% OF SWISS WINE IS
EXPORTED. IN ADDITION,
SWITZERLAND IMPORTS MORE
WINE THAN IT PRODUCES.

WINE IMPORTED:
**183**
MILLION LITRES

## GROWERS-PRODUCERS

**15,000 VIGNERONS**
OF WHICH MORE THAN HALF
ARE NON-PROFESSIONALS

# VINEYARDS

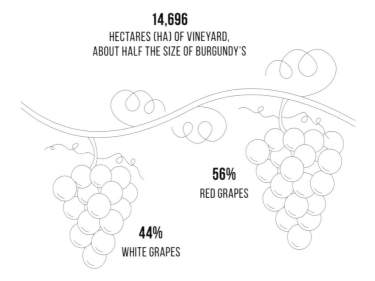

**14,696**
HECTARES (HA) OF VINEYARD,
ABOUT HALF THE SIZE OF BURGUNDY'S

**56%**
RED GRAPES

**44%**
WHITE GRAPES

# REGIONS

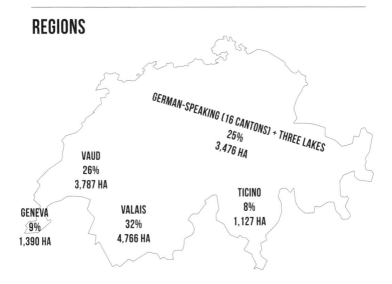

GERMAN-SPEAKING (16 CANTONS) + THREE LAKES
25%
3,476 HA

VAUD
26%
3,787 HA

TICINO
8%
1,127 HA

GENEVA
9%
1,390 HA

VALAIS
32%
4,766 HA

**Sources:**
Swiss Wine Year 2020, Federal Office for Agriculture
OIV (International Organisation of Vine and Wine)

# WINERY ETIQUETTE, WINE-SPEAK

- You can taste wine without buying it, but be gracious and order one or three bottles to be shipped, which is easy in Switzerland.

- There is no set rule for paying for tasting. In the past most wineries offered this for free, but clients tended to be local and they would buy their annual supply of wine. Today, you can expect to be charged CHF15-25 to taste 4-6 wines in many wineries, and where they are equipped to offer more, you might be given the option to have wine with a snack or to tour the winery as part of their effort to educate consumers. Small wineries that are run by one person or a couple simply don't have the time and the means to offer regular tasting sessions, but if you do contact them to make an appointment, it is usually free of charge.

- Do spit out and don't worry about how it looks or sounds – it's the only way to taste more than one wine. Save any drinking for the end.

- Three keys to judging a wine are: what it looks like, what it smells like, what it tastes like. Don't worry about the fancy language swirling around all this. Ask yourself if you like all three aspects of it. When the vigneron asks you if you like it, be honest. They really do want to know.

- Do ask the vigneron to describe the smell and taste and take home a little new knowledge.

- Do ask how the wine is made. Switzerland's artisanal wineries are a showcase for precision, discretion, and a vision that calls for products tied closely to their place of origin. Vignerons want to share what they learn as they "accompany" the grapes on the journey from vine to bottle.

- Brush up on basic vocabulary. Switzerland pioneered **integrated production** (IP) agriculture in the 1990s for a better relationship with the environment and today there is a strong movement to take this further, with many wineries "**reconverting**" to **organic** (bio) and **biodynamic** (a method but also a philosophy). There's a strong focus on preserving the **soil**, which is key for perfect grapes. Switzerland has a wide variety of **soil types** and these play a key role in defining a **terroir**. Once the grapes are harvested they are pressed and **vinified**, meaning turned into an alcoholic beverage through

**fermentation**. Once the juice becomes wine, it needs to **mature**, sometimes in stainless steel or cement **tanks**, sometimes in **oak containers** of various sizes (barrels, vats, casks). Ask when the wine is **bottled**, which normally varies from January to August following the harvest, although it can be much later. Ask how to read the **label**. And know that all along the way, as the vigneron accompanies the grapes and the wine, scores of decisions have to be made that have an impact on the end result. These wines are not industrial products, but a gift from the land, created with hard work and a good deal of love.

- **Vigneron (vee-nyur-own)**, interchangeable with wine producer. The word comes from French but is used in other languages, including English. In Switzerland it generally means someone who cultivates the grapes and then vinifies them. There are also growers, who turn their grapes over to someone else to make into wine, either a cooperative or a consultant vigneron or winemaker. A winemaker is usually a trained **oenologist**, but the term implies that someone else takes care of the work in the vineyard. Vintner is another term used in other countries but it lacks precision to describe Switzerland's approach to making wine, so vigneron is more widely used. Note that in French **vigneronne** is now widely used for the rapidly growing number of women who are grower/producers.

# 3

# MAP & INDEX

# MAP

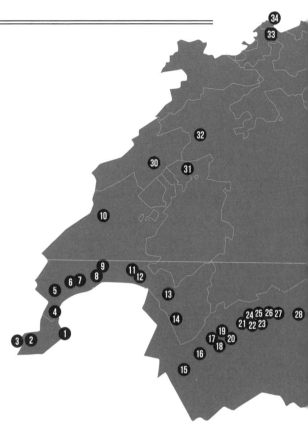

# HIKES

| NAME OF THE ROUTE | STARTING POINT | LENGTH | MAP |
|---|---|---|---|
| Aran-Villette | Chexbres | 8.2 km | 11 |
| Capolago | Besazio | 8.7 km | 50 |
| Croglio-Castelrotto | Novaggio | 8.5 km | 47 |
| Cully | Vevey | 12.8 km | 12 |
| Dardagny | Peissy | 12.2 km | 3 |
| Échichens | Saint-Prex | 11.7 km | 9 |
| Eglisau | Eglisau | 11.4 km | 38 |
| Erlinsbach | Wittnau | 8.6 km | 35 |
| Féchy | Aubonne | 8.3 km | 7 |
| Flanthey | Granges | 11.1 km | 21 |
| Founex | Céligny | 10.3 km | 4 |
| Fully | Branson | 11.7 km | 16 |
| Givrins | Vich | 10.6 km | 5 |
| Jenins | Fläsch | 8.5 km | 42 |
| Jussy | Hermance | 12.7 km | 1 |
| Kastanienbaum | Stansstad | 9 km | 45 |
| Küttigen | Salhöhe | 10.9 km | 36 |
| Leuk | Bratsch | 9.6 km | 27 |
| Lugano | Riva Cantonetto di Gentilino | 7 km | 48 |
| Maienfeld | Bad Ragaz | 15.5 km | 41 |
| Malans | Malans | 12.3 km | 44 |
| Malans | Malans | 7.3 km | 43 |
| Martigny-Combe | Martigny Croix | 7.4 km | 15 |
| Meilen | Forch | 14.2 km | 39 |
| Milvignes | Bevaix | 10.35 km | 30 |
| Monte Carasso | Monte Carasso | 10 km | 46 |
| Morcote | Paradiso | 11.8 km | 49 |
| Môtier-Vully | Murten | 10.9 km | 31 |
| Muttenz | Liestal | 10.6 km | 33 |
| Ollon | Yvorne | 9.8 km | 14 |
| Raron | Ausserberg | 10.9 km | 28 |
| Riehen | Basel | 10.4 km | 34 |
| Saint-Pierre-de-Clages | Saillon | 13.1 km | 17 |
| Saint-Pierre-de-Clages | Chamoson | 11 km | 18 |
| Saint-Prex | Etoy | 6.8 km | 8 |
| Salgesch | Sierre | 22.6 km | 26 |
| Satigny | Satigny | 8.8 km | 2 |
| Sierre Muraz | Colombire | 12.3 km | 24 |
| Sierre | Chalais | 12 km | 23 |
| Sierre | Grimisuat | 19.9 km | 22 |
| Sion | Drône | 10.3 km | 20 |
| Tartegnin | Rolle | 9.3 km | 6 |
| Thal | Heiden | 7.7 km | 40 |
| Twann | Neuveville | 8.3 km | 32 |
| Untersiggenthal | Kirchdorf | 13.3 km | 37 |
| Valeyres | Romainmôtier | 13 km | 10 |
| Venthône | Veyras | 10.3 km | 25 |
| Vétroz | Chandolin | 13.1 km | 19 |
| Villeneuve | Saint-Gingolph | 13.6 km | 13 |
| Visperterminen | Visperterminen | 6.8 km | 29 |

# WINERIES & WINES

# 4

# THE WINE HIKES

# GENEVA

# JUSSY

## WALKING THE LINE, LITERALLY, WITH OLD FRANCE

ENTRE ARVE
ET LAC

▷⋯ STARTING POINT

**HERMANCE
END OF LINE BUS STOP**

⋯✕ DESTINATION

**JUSSY
VINS DE LA GARA**

📅 SEASON

**YEAR-ROUND**

🗺 HIKE TYPE

**EASY** 🚶

🗺 MAP REFERENCE

**SHEET 270T**

⏱ DURATION

**3H 15M**

↦ LENGTH

**12.7 KM**

🔍 INTERESTING SIGHTS

OLD TOWN OF HERMANCE. 19TH CENTURY
ARCHITECTURE AND LAKEFRONT FISHING HUT.
CANTON GENEVA'S TERROIR FOOD FARMS.
VIEW OF MONT BLANC. JUSSY'S THREE CHATEAUS.

〰 CLIMB / DESCENT

**227 M / 142 M**

| | |
|---|---|
| CHARDONNAY | CHARDONNAY<br>VINS DE LA GARA |
| WHITE | |
| WHITE FLOWERS,<br>CITRUS FRUITS,<br>NOTABLY MINERAL | |
| DRY AND DELICATE,<br>MINERAL AND<br>LIGHTLY FRUITY | |
| DRY,<br>STILL | |

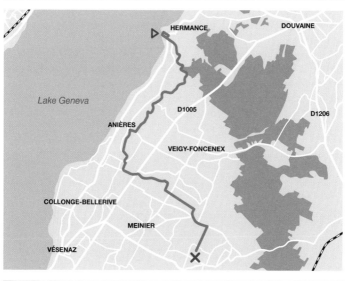

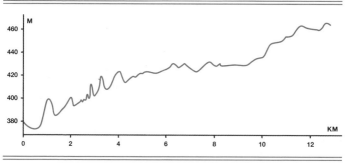

# DESCRIPTION OF THE ROUTE

The bus line ends at a turnaround point in Hermance with good information about hiking in the region at the bus shelter. From here, explore the center of this old village on the border with France and walk to the lakefront: follow Route d'Hermance in the direction of the border (away from the city of Geneva), turn left and walk down Rue Centrale to Ruelle des Galeries and turn left at the end to reach the small beach and waterfront walkway. Just beyond the beach is the point where the Hermance River feeds into Lake Geneva.

Head left along the lake to return to the bus shelter by turning left at the fishing hut and shop, easily spotted thanks to colourful nets and fishing paraphernalia. Follow Chemin des Fossés to the bus parking area and continue straight, uphill, on what is now called Chemin Crêt-de-la-Tour. The street bends right. Continue straight to the fork in the road with Route de Chevrens, the main street that continues to the right. Instead, take the smaller path left, Chemin des Chenaillettes. This is the start of an area that is heaven for hikers and dog-walkers on weekends and holidays, since cars are banned and these small roads are reserved for those on foot. The trail goes through open woods parallel and close to the winding little Hermance River that serves as the border with France. Continue to follow the marked footpath for a good distance; at Croix de Bally there is a fork to the right (ignore it) and a little further a small road and a footpath to the right (ignore these), but otherwise there are no turnoffs from the trail until a small road and farmhouse at Les Tattes, just before the farm village of Chevrens. Continue to follow the marked footpath, staying close to the river, until just after Chevrens, which is on the right.

The marked footpath separates into two strands at Les Cheneviers: take the right hand path. It is possible to continue on the left to the end of the trail, at the French border, but that requires walking along a busy road. The trail here takes the small farm road on the right and begins to follow fields and a little further on, vineyards. There are signs everywhere for *Genève Terroir* local farm products. When the road turns right and stops at Chemin de Boret, take a left and continue on this road until it ends at Chemin des Champs-Nabez. Take a right and immediately turn left onto a footpath that goes behind L'Abbaye. When the path ends, turn right onto Route de l'Hospice. Shortly after the cemetery on the right, turn left along a footpath that continues along the top of a vineyard. When the vines end turn left onto Route de la Côte d'Or, which bends right to cross over the Nant d'Aisy, a small river. At a T-junction turn left, then right onto Chemin du Château: the street cuts through the center of the farm town of Corsier. Turn left at Route de l'Eglise and continue to a roundabout. Take the second street (the first is smaller) which turns into a footpath that continues along the small river. Follow this for half a kilometre until just before the hamlet of Veigy, and take the footpath to the right. It takes a sharp left turn and

continues to the village of Gy. Turn right onto the main street, then left shortly before the roundabout and follow signs for Jussy.

After a small farm on the right, take the next right along a road which leads past fields, a small vineyard and over the little Le Chambet river straight to La Gara.

**Return**
A 5-10 minute walk to any of several bus stops.

**Notes**
Hermance is a wonderful destination via Lake Geneva CGN steamboat, which offers a nice idea of the shoreline and the gentle rise towards the French Alps – on a clear day you can see Mt. Blanc. This is a very good walk with dogs with easy wide paths, some of which are closed to traffic on weekends and holidays. Expect to have company: this is the country but close to the city, a major source of food to Geneva's urban population.

# VINS DE LA GARA

This is a small but very special winery, not visible to the public because it is part of a beautiful 18th century home known for its formal gardens and labyrinth, enclosed within high gates. The winery and the gardens both require appointments for visits; it is worthwhile to do both. The gardens were restored in 2000 and are worked using permaculture. The canal, the only such 18th century canal in Switzerland, was restored in 2015 when the labyrinth was also built. Wine has been made here from 3 hectares of vines cultivated around the manor house since 1753. Winemaker Adeline Wegmüller trained in Switzerland, France and New Zealand; she has been at the winery since 2020, but she is making her mark with elegant wines notable for their pure, clean lines and delicate colours. The wines are made in the cellar of the mansion. Good value for money.

 **Chardonnay:** A clear idea from this young winemaker of what a good unoaked Chardonnay should give, starting with the very pale yellow colour – the fruit is there and it's well made.

## ADDRESS

**Vins de la Gara**
Rte de la Gara 36
1254 Jussy
Tel: 079 647 4257
awegmuller@lagara.ch
For the La Gara gardens: lesjardins@lagara.ch
lagara.ch

## WINERY FEES

No, but essential to reserve.

## WHERE ELSE TO FIND THIS CELLAR'S WINES NEARBY

**Auberge de la Couronne**, Rte de Jussy 316, 1254 Jussy,
022 759 12 66
reservation@aubergecouronne.com

# SATIGNY

## GENEVA BEYOND THE CITY: SWITZERLAND'S LARGEST VINEYARD

RIVE DROITE

| ▷⋯ STARTING POINT | ⋯✗ DESTINATION |
|---|---|
| **SATIGNY TRAIN STATION** | **DOMAINE GRAND CLOS, SATIGNY** |
| 📅 SEASON | HIKE TYPE |
| **YEAR-ROUND** | **EASY** 🚶 |
| ⛰ MAP REFERENCE | ⏱ DURATION |
| **SHEET 261T** | **2H 15M** |
| | ↦ LENGTH |
| 🔍 INTERESTING SIGHTS | **8.8 KM** |
| BUCOLIC GENEVA COUNTRYSIDE. VIEWS OF JURA AND FRENCH/SWISS ALPS. MANOR HOUSES. | 〰 CLIMB / DESCENT |
| | **183 M / 183 M** |

# ICONIQUE
# SAUVIGNON
## WINERY GRAND CLOS

WHITE

SLOWLY UNFOLDING AND
INTENSE NOTES
OF GRAPEFRUIT, LIME,
SAGE, EXOTIC FRUITS

CRISP, MINERAL,
SLIGHTLY SALTY,
REFRESHING

DRY,
STILL

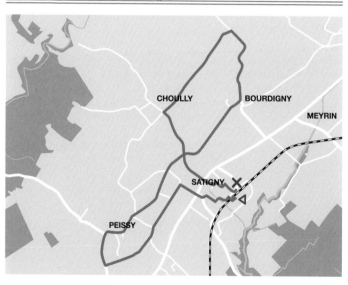

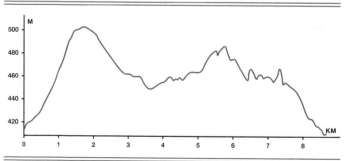

# DESCRIPTION OF THE ROUTE

A bucolic ramble through the wine villages of Geneva where it's easy to forget what century you're in, once you leave the train station in Satigny (from Geneva main station, take semi-hidden track 5). Walk straight uphill to Choully and you're immediately in the heart of Switzerland's largest wine-producing commune, Satigny, where you are surrounded by vines.

Turn right onto Route du Crêt-de-Choully and continue, then right again and downhill into the hamlet of Bourdigny, past organic farms that are a popular source of direct marketing for Geneva's sustainability-minded population. Head back towards the top end of Satigny village, but follow signs to Peissy, one of the prettiest of the villages, and home to a number of top Geneva wineries. Frequent visitors from the city tasting and buying wine make this a lively place. The main street dips down to the right. At the bottom of the hill there's a useful wooden pillar that lists wine aromas, compliments of *Genève Terroir*, the cantonal agriculture office. For future hiking plans, the road straight ahead is part of a lengthy cantonal hiking trail with several educational panels like this.

Instead, follow signs to the left for Russin, where you're back in quiet working vineyard country. The road rises and dips over a few hundred metres. Don't follow the road to the bottom of the hill and a busy intersection. Instead, cut left across farm vehicle tracks that take you back to Satigny, domaine Grand Clos (route du Mandement) and the train

station. Stay on the broad tractor trails – don't wander through the vines. Vineyard rows are not simply unmowed or wild but are planted with useful cover crops. They are home to rich bird and animal life, such as hares, which nest on the ground. Geneva's vignerons are working hard to make the transition to organic and biodynamic farming and the canton has a reputation for respecting its wealth of wildlife.

**Return**
Five-minute walk to Satigny train station.

**Notes**
The string of villages on the trail earned contemporary fame in the 1980s when they held Switzerland's first hugely popular wineries open house day – a phenomenon that quickly caught on in other wine

regions. For those unaware, it comes as a surprise that Satigny is Switzerland's largest vineyard commune, an area that covers much more than the village itself.

Choully is a typical "Mandement" village, as is Bourdigny, with centuries-old manor houses behind high walls and glimpses of busy courtyards of many of the houses, working wineries. Satigny is a municipality that covers most of the old Mandement, an area that is a listed Swiss Heritage site. Geneva's oldest authenticated historical document refers to a donation of these villages to the monastery of St. Peter, although the owner insisted the bishop ensure that her right to *usufruit* (use of the land) was respected. Over the centuries land here was traded and swapped and donated by bishops, monks and countesses, as part of numerous storied religious squabbles. The villages are part of the foothills of the French Jura and thus overlook the city of Geneva. Historical ties to France remain close. Urban Geneva appears so near and yet, when hiking, so comfortingly far away, with noise and bustle soon forgotten. At Bourdigny it is possible to continue on a longer hiking loop straight ahead to CERN (the large white complex is visible from the trail), the European Organisation for Nuclear Research, home to the Large Hadron Collider. Starting near the trail, the LHC's enormous circular collider runs underground towards France.

Despite its big reputation, the winery's shopfront on the main street in Satigny is small and not easy to spot.

This walk can readily be combined with part or all of the longer Peissy to Dardagny hike if you want to spend a long day on the trail.

# DOMAINE GRAND CLOS JEAN-MICHEL NOVELLE

Grand Clos is the official name of this family winery, but outlier Jean-Michel Novelle has gained such a reputation for his wines that people often think Novelle is the name of the winery. He spent years working in South America and France, while continuing to work in Geneva, all the while developing a fiercely purist philosophy about cultivating grapes and making wines of great character. He produces an astonishing 38 wines from 17 grape varieties, with many of the grapes part of what he refers to as his experimental laboratory. The *Iconique* line of wines focuses on producing single grape wines where you can almost hear the fruit sing, the notes are so pure.

**Iconique Sauvignon:** all attention is on the grape and its fruity profile, a classic from this innovator.

## ADDRESS

**Winery Grand Clos**
Route du Mandement 153
1242 Satigny-Geneva
022 753 1009 or 079 596 6753
contact@novelle.wine
By appointment

## WINERY FEES

Several options

## WHERE ELSE TO FIND THIS CELLAR'S WINES NEARBY

**Domaine de Châteauvieux**, Peney-Dessus 16, 1242 Satigny,
022 753 15 11
reservation@chateauvieux.ch
**Le Renfort**, Rte du Creux-du-Loup 19, 1285 Avusy,
022 756 12 36
See list on the winery's website

# DARDAGNY

## GENÈVE TERROIR IN ITS GLORY, WHERE EVERYTHING GROWS

RIVE DROITE

| ▷··· STARTING POINT | ···✕ DESTINATION |
|---|---|
| PEISSY<br>BUS STOP | DOMAINE DE CHAFALET,<br>DARDAGNY (ESSERTINES) |

| 📅 SEASON | 🗓 HIKE TYPE |
|---|---|
| YEAR-ROUND | EASY |

| 🗺 MAP REFERENCE | ⏱ DURATION |
|---|---|
| SHEET 270T | 3H 10M |

| | ↦ LENGTH |
|---|---|
| | 12.2 KM |

| 🔍 INTERESTING SIGHTS | 〽 CLIMB / DESCENT |
|---|---|
| ALLONDON NATURE RESERVE.<br>CLASSIC MANDEMENT WINE VILLAGES.<br>CHATEAU WHERE MOZART SPENT TIME.<br>SYLVIE RAMU SCULPTURES. | 275 M / 303 M |

SYRAH

# SHÉHÉRAZADE
### DOMAINE DE CHAFALET

RED

FLORAL,
SPICY

FRESH, SILKY,
SUBTLY OAKED,
LONG FINISH

DRY,
STILL

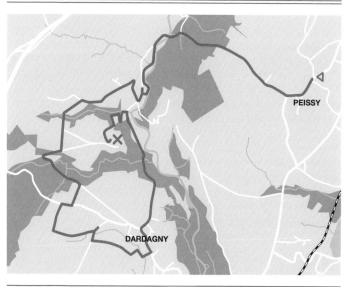

PEISSY

DARDAGNY

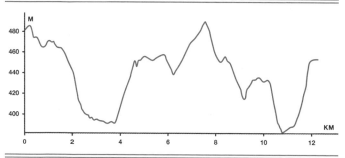

# DESCRIPTION OF THE ROUTE

Follow the road from the bus stop along Peissy's main street, through vineyards and fields of cereals, and past cellars of some of Geneva's best-known wineries. Geneva is proud of its record for sustainability, wildlife protection and mixed farming, and it is all at work in this area. The road leads to the Grand Bois at the start of the Allondon Nature Reserve; before entering the woods, a trail leads to the left, which is a large loop through the woods that hooks back up with this trail. The trail follows the road.

Head gently downhill towards the Allondon river and bear left after crossing it. Initially stay on the road, then follow the footpath signs that lead to the lightly wooded riverside. This is a popular area for dog walking, school and corporate educational outings, so there are several nature trails; follow the signs for the trail close to the river until you reach the Allondon Center At this point turn left and follow the road briefly to an intersection with a bus stop; turn right onto the road that leads to Malval. It skirts the hilltop where the hamlet of Essertines sits, including the winery, whose name comes from Chafale, the name of an old border customs observation post for watching commercial traffic.

The trail continues on towards Dardagny, one of the main Mandement wine villages. Soon after the collection of buildings that is Malval, turn left onto a marked trail through the vines, along Route de Malval, crossing over the road that leads into Essertines until you reach a T-junction. Turn right; this is still the Route de Malval (which has bus service). Follow marked hiking signs that include several turns as the trail moves through vineyards and fields, leading into Dardagny.

The village is long and the trail arrives at the bottom end, just below the chateau where music composer Mozart began a major Swiss tour in 1766. Turn left and follow the main street uphill to the central square where the trail heads right at the top end. A quiet road out of town goes along a ridge with a fine view of distant Geneva, down a wooded stretch of road into the Vallon de l'Allondon and to signs for Essertines and the winery.

**Return**
Essertine bus stop to La Plaine train station

**Notes**
In order to rejoin the start of the trail, it's possible to walk from the Satigny train station, following the road taken by the bus. It adds 4.5 km of easy walking and one hour to the trail, while avoiding a wait for the bus.

Essertines and Dardagny are home to several Ramu families who all make award-winning wines; be sure to look for signs with this winery's name, Chafalet.

# DOMAINE DE CHAFALET

This is one of the liveliest family domains around, with the atelier for mother and artist Sylvie Ramu's well-known sculptures in one corner, various activities linked to the seven adult children sprinkled around the domaine, stables and horses as a separate but central part of the larger operations – and of course the winery. Mathurin joined his father at age 17 to make wines and now, at the ripe old age of 30 (in 2022), is in charge of vines and wines; he is a whirlwind of activity, winning awards while retaining his youthful enthusiasm and good cheer. Irreverent fun combined with classy wines.

 **Shéhérazade:** Well-ripened grapes. One more fine example in the growing collection of Swiss Rhone valley Syrahs, just north of the famous French Northern Rhones.

## ADDRESS

**Domaine de Chafalet**
Chemin du Chafalet 16
1283 Essertines
Tel: 079 364 6599
mathurin@chafalet.ch
chafalet.ch

## WINERY FEES

No

## WHERE ELSE TO FIND THIS CELLAR'S WINES NEARBY

**Auberge de Dardagny**, Rte du Mandement 504, 1283 Dardagny, 022 754 14 72

# VAUD

# FOUNEX

## GENTLE FARMS, 17TH C. CASTLES, MEDIEVAL TOWN

TERRE SAINTE

| ▷⋯ STARTING POINT | ⋯✕ DESTINATION |
|---|---|
| **CÉLIGNY VILLAGE (BUS STOP AT SQUARE WITH FOUNTAIN)** | **LES FRÈRES DUTRUY, FOUNEX** |

| 🗓 SEASON | 🏁 HIKE TYPE |
|---|---|
| **YEAR-ROUND** | **EASY** |

| 🗺 MAP REFERENCE | ⏱ DURATION |
|---|---|
| **SHEET 270T** | **2H 30M** |
| | ↦ LENGTH |
| 🔍 INTERESTING SIGHTS | **10.3 KM** |
| CHÂTEAU GARENGO. CHÂTEAU DE BOSSEY. CHÂTEAU DE COPPET AND MEDIEVAL TOWN OF COPPET. VILLAGE OF FOUNEX. | 〰 CLIMB / DESCENT |
| | **119 M / 152 M** |

# GAMAY LES ROMAINES
## LES FRÈRES DUTRUY

 RED

 CHERRIES AND BLUEBERRIES,
SPICES,
FLORAL — VIOLET AND IRIS

 COMPLEX AND VERY LONG

 DRY,
STILL,
OAKED

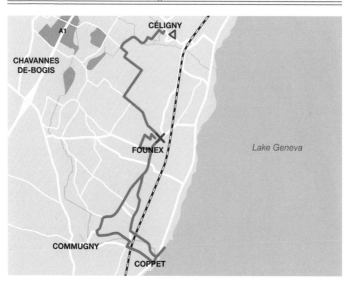

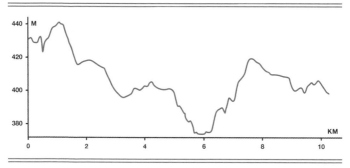

# DESCRIPTION OF THE ROUTE

The bus stops in front of Céligny's Protestant temple, a Romanesque church with an architecturally unusual clock tower wall, and an 18th century private chateau with formal gardens and courtyard. The village sets the tone for the walk through this Vaud-Geneva (Céligny is a Geneva enclave) countryside that recalls medieval to 18th century agriculture and architecture. The trail turns left from these buildings and heads uphill briefly; turn left at signs for the Château de Bossey. The trail leads through light woodland and fields, around the large and typical 18th century farm aptly named Belle Ferme.

The trail meets up with the Way of St. James of Compostello at the renovated Château de Bossey, built in 1722. It is home to the Ecumenical Institute of the World Council of Churches. Below the chateau turn

right onto Chemin Chenevière, then left, following footpath signs to Founex. Follow the yellow arrows to the right along a footpath, with Belle Ferme behind now. At the T-junction turn left onto Chemin de Pacoty and follow it to the end at the Grand'Rue in Founex.

Turn right onto this charming narrow main street. Continue until the road splits at Route de Founex with vineyards now on the left. Follow the road through a residential area, downhill until a small street, Le Chemin Bleu. Turn left and continue down. The name changes twice before the trail comes out on the grounds side of the chateau in Coppet. Turn left onto Route Suisse, which is also the main street of Coppet. Cross the road, and go right along the Chemin des jardins to reach the lakefront, with its small dock.

Retrace steps to the Route Suisse, also named Grand'Rue, and walk in the direction of Geneva (marked). The old Coppet museum (Musée du Vieux Coppet) is on the right; continue to Rue du Perron and turn right, then left at the end of the street onto Rue du Greny which joins Rue des Murs just below the chateau on the right. Turn up the road in front of it.

Walk uphill and past the railway line to turn right at Route de Founex. Take the first left onto Chemin du Clos and continue past a vineyard on the left, until a T-junction with Route de l'Église. Turn right and follow as the road bends left. Then turn right onto Route de Founex and carry on for some distance – it becomes the Route du Jura – and rejoin the route taken earlier. At the Grand'Rue turn left up the Route de Chataigneriaz. Turn right onto a farm road, Chemin des Fancous, then walk down Chemin des Hutins, on a small farm path to the right. Turn left at Chemin de la Treille. The second right leads to the winery's back entrance and nursery, and the main street of Founex.

**Return**
Founex's main street is well served by buses.

**Notes**
This relatively flat stroll through the Vaud countryside of gentle agricultural scenes (expect stables and horses, sheep, cereal crops, vines) is complemented by a walk through the medieval town of Coppet on the lakefront. The trail passes by the front of the winery before heading down to the lake. It is possible to turn this into a much shorter walk, about half the length, by eliminating the visit to Coppet. For groups with hikers of varying ability, the option to leave some people at the winery sooner might be useful.

Note that the CGN steamboat dock in Coppet is below the chateau.

# LES FRÈRES DUTRUY

The Dutruy family in 2017 celebrated 100 years and four generations of making wine here, barely pausing to rest on their laurels. Despite its size, this artisanal operation is one of canton Vaud's 20th century winemaking success stories. They were compensated in 2017 by being named Swiss Winery of the Year by the national Grand Prix des Vins Suisses. Brothers Julien and Christian began collaborating young after each spent time abroad, training and working in wineries in several countries. One oversees the vineyards, the other winemaking, but they also have a vine nursery: the combination gives them a high level of expertise in grapes and terroir that is clear in the wines they produce.

 **Gamay Les Romaines:** Les Romaines is the winery's group of top-line wines here, all matured in oak for at least a year. Compare this Gamay of wonderful depth to the winery's very good but more ordinary Gamay at half the price (made in stainless steel tanks) to understand the difference.

## ADDRESS

**Les Frères Dutruy**
Grand-Rue 18
1297 Founex
Tel: 022 776 5402
dutruy@lesfreresdutruy.ch
lesfreresdutruy.ch/contact/

## WINERY FEES

No. Tastings generally possible during business hours and Saturday mornings.

## WHERE ELSE TO FIND THIS CELLAR'S WINES NEARBY

**Auberge de Founex**, Grand-Rue 31, 1297 Founex,
022 776 10 29
aubergedefounex@bluewin.ch
**L'Intemporel**, Grand-Rue 6, 1297 Founex,
076 360 29 78
reservation@lintemporel.ch
**Hôtel Everness**, Les Champs-Blancs 70b, 1279 Chavannes-de-Bogis,
022 960 81 81

# GIVRINS

## WORLD WAR 2 RIVERSIDE TOBLERONES

TERRE SAINTE

| ▷⋯ STARTING POINT | ⋯✗ DESTINATION |
|---|---|
| **VICH,** **POST OFFICE BUS STOP** | **CAVE PHILIPPE BOVET,** **GIVRINS** |
| 🗓 SEASON | 🔀 HIKE TYPE |
| **YEAR-ROUND** | **EASY** 🚶 |
| 🗺 MAP REFERENCE | 🕐 DURATION |
| | **2H 45M** |
| **SHEET 460T** | ↦ LENGTH |
| | **10.6 KM** |
| 🔍 INTERESTING SIGHTS | 〰 CLIMB / DESCENT |
| TOBLERONE TRAIL (WW2 DEFENSIVE LINE, NOT CHOCOLATE!). GENOLIER FERME DU BOIS DE CHÊNE. | **330 M / 223 M** |

# MERLOT
CAVE PHILIPPE BOVET

 RED

 BLACK FRUITS, LICORICE, TOASTING NOTES, CHOCOLATE, PEPPER

 RICH AND POWERFUL, BLACKCURRANT AND CHERRIES, A BIG AND LUSCIOUS WINE

 DRY, STILL

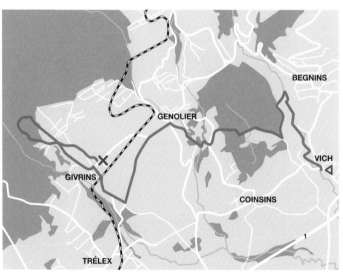

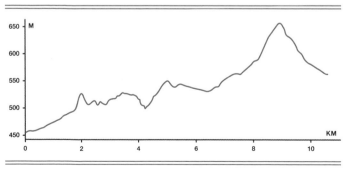

# DESCRIPTION OF THE ROUTE

From the Vich post office bus stop, head along the Route de Begnins, looking for the well-marked number 114 Sentier des Toblerones trail to the left. It is 18 km but our trail follows only part of it. Most of the walk here is along a small river, with educational information about the idea behind these "toblerones". At one point the trail crosses the Serine river with vineyards on the right. It crosses back a second time. Near the entrance to Begnins, at La Crosette, take a sharp left, crossing the river a third time. There are two more intersections before reaching Château Grillet: stay left each time (the second time the trail becomes a road) and at Château Grillet take a very sharp right and follow the trail to Ferme du Bois de Chêne.

Go past the Ferme du Bois de Chêne, continuing on the road as it bends right through the woods. Coming out of the woods take the small footpath to the left just before the Y-junction. When it ends, cross the road and follow the footpath briefly through woods and across a stream, coming out at the edge of Genolier. Turn right, keeping the large farm buildings on the left and go around them, past a road to the right, to an intersection. Turn right onto Chemin de la Brégentenaz and then right at Route de Duillier. Make a loop to the left around the town plaza.

Follow straight along the Route de Trélex. This is not a very busy road, but there are no sidewalks and there is some traffic. The trail follows

the road for about 1.5 km. At the four-way intersection turn right onto the Route de Duillier towards the center of Givrins. After a farm on the left, the road dips down to join the Route de Trélex. Follow this into the center of the village – note that the winery is quite close, on the right, but the trail will return here later. (If you want to skip 2 km of hiking, you can simply go to the winery, to the right about 100 m.)

For those staying on the trail: from the roundabout, turn left, then right onto Route de la Scie. Go right onto Chemin des Epinettes. Follow it to the intersection with Route du Stand and turn left along the small road, Chemin en Pont Trembley. Shortly after Chemin des Oiseaux the road becomes a footpath. Stay on this and when it splits take the right-hand path to begin the loop back to Givrins. A trail comes in from the left, then another and immediately after this take the left-hand split to go onto Chemin du Pré-de-la-Maison. Immediately after this turn right onto the footpath, Rue du Stand.

Follow this right back to the edge of Givrins. The road splits at the entrance to the village. Take the left option, Chemin du Carré, a street that looks like an alley. Follow it and keep a careful eye out for signs for the winery on the right. The winery can also be entered via a courtyard off the Route de Genolier.

**Return**
The Givrins local line train station is a 10-minute walk. The bus stop is two minutes from the winery.

**Notes**
It's possible to spend years in this area and think it is mainly a home for horses, cows, vines and grains, when in fact it sits in deep layers of regional history. The Toblerone Trail, of which just one part is included here, takes hikers on a tour of some of the 3,000 concrete triangles (each the height of a man) along a 10 km line between the Jura foothills and Lake Geneva. The toblerones (named for the chocolate, which came first) were built along rivers and streams, starting in 1940 when Germany attacked other neutral countries, Belgium and Norway. After the war some were restored and today the trail is like a living museum, with educational panels.

Close by the Bois de Chêne are important ruins from an earlier time: Le Molard/Molar was a fortified fort surrounded by a circular moat typical of its tlme (c.1210). Predecessors were part of the entourage of 10th century kings of Burgundy. For more than a millennium this area has been a wealthy agricultural stronghold and Bois de Chêne was one of the most important places in the area.

# CAVE PHILIPPE BOVET

Philippe Bovet is as well known for his creative energy as the quality of his wines. He has worked as a consultant for several cellars in the area, all the while building his own winery (opened in 2002). The range of wines is interesting and large. This very fun winemaker is an avid supporter of several sports teams, and the wines are excellent. When the region suffered huge losses from a historic hail storm in 2013 – he lost 95% of his grapes that June – he rushed to buy grapes from elsewhere and marketed the emergency wine blend by giving it the date of the storm and using the last-second weather forecast for the label.

**Merlot:** Philippe Bovet was one of the first to insist that Merlot could do well in this part of Switzerland. Ask about his other very special Merlot, A Mon Rhône.

## ADDRESS

**Cave Philippe Bovet**
La Cour, Route de Genolier 7
1271 Givrins
Tel: 022 369 3814
Mobile: 079 445 8730
info@philippebovet.ch
philippebovet.ch

## WINERY FEES

No. Regular hours.

## WHERE ELSE TO FIND THIS CELLAR'S WINES NEARBY

**Auberge Communale au Sapins**, Rte de Genolier 1, 1271 Givrins, 022 369 18 01
nathaly.michaud@bluewin.ch

# TARTEGNIN

## SEVEN CENTURIES OF CASTLES AND WINE

LA CÔTE

| | |
|---|---|
| ▷··· STARTING POINT | ···✕ DESTINATION |
| **ROLLE TRAIN STATION** | **DOMAINE DE PENLOUP, TARTEGNIN** |
| 🗓 SEASON | ▦ HIKE TYPE |
| **YEAR-ROUND** | **MODERATE** 🚶 |
| ⛰ MAP REFERENCE | 🕐 DURATION |
| | **2H 45M** |
| **SHEET 460T** | ↦ LENGTH |
| | **9.3 KM** |
| 🔍 INTERESTING SIGHTS | |
| 11TH CENTURY CASTLE VINCY. LE ROSEY CONTEMPORARY CARNAL HALL CENTER FOR THE PERFORMING ARTS. LA CHATAGNERÉAZ. CHÂTEAU DE MONT DE VIEUX RUINS. | ∿ CLIMB / DESCENT |
| | **412 M / 294 M** |

# PINOT BLANC PUR
## DOMAINES DE PENLOUP AND ES CORDELIÈRES

 WHITE

 CITRUS FRUITS

 FRESH, MOUTH-FILLING

 DRY, STILL

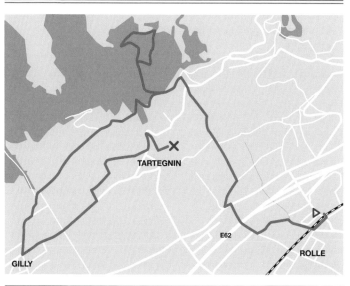

TARTEGNIN

E62

GILLY

ROLLE

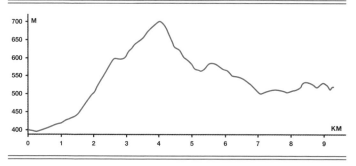

# DESCRIPTION OF THE ROUTE

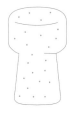

From the train station in Rolle, head in the direction of Geneva taking either of the footpaths that run along each side of the tracks, then go right up a footpath on the northwest side of the tracks until you come to the path called Route des Quatre Communes, which shortly turns into a small road.  Stay on it as it bends sharply and makes a hairpin turn: it is the road that runs next to Le Rosey, a 150-year-old school interesting due to its old and new architecture as well as its reputation as "the school of kings" – and as one of the world's most expensive secondary schools. Follow the road, continuing straight, over the autoroute. Turn left at the roundabout, cross Route de l'Etraz and immediately take the first right, heading uphill onto Route du Creux-du-Mas.

Take the second left, the Chemin de Chatagneréaz and start walking steadily uphill. The castle at Chatagneréaz on the left has served as a cellar for more than 1,000 years, with owners who varied from religious orders to wealthy *seigneurs* depending on how the religious, political and economic winds were blowing. Today the castle has some of the best vineyards in the region. Keep walking uphill until you reach the old chestnut tree forest above the vineyards.

At the hamlet of Bugnaux take a left then the first right and continue to climb, following the footpath, alongside the ruins of the Château Mont-le-Vieux, once the powerful seat of the towns in this area. Turn left at the ruins and follow Route de Châtel in a loop back down to Bugnaux. Shortly before the village there is a sharp right, La Rommaz. Follow the road past a couple of buildings; take the trail off the road to the right and follow it over Le Ruisseau de Famolens. The trail rejoins the road to Vincy, called first Chemin de la Bossenaz, then Route du Pavillon. The road has signs for the Gilly hospital, which is uphill on the right.

Continue to Vincy, a small collection of houses dominated by its chateau, surprisingly the home of one of the world's most famous contemporary architects, Norman Foster. The land and vineyards are part of one of the oldest *seigneuries* around Lake Geneva. The trail here starts downhill then turns left to loop around the castle. The rest of the hike is through vineyards, following one of several parallel paths. Any of these could be taken, but the trail towards the end, in Tartegnin, heads steeply uphill, so it's easiest not to go too far downhill in Vincy.

In Tartegnin, follow signs in the center of the village for Domaine Penloup.

**Return**
Bus service from the center of Tartegnin operates between Gland and Rolle train stations.

## Notes

There is a long uphill trek at the outset, but the view alone is worth it, with much of La Côte's vineyards spread out below and clear views for most of the length of Lake Geneva.

# DOMAINES DE PENLOUP AND ES CORDELIÈRES

The main winery, Penloup, has belonged to the Graenicher family since 1983, making them relative newcomers in this region of millennial-old vineyards, but they've made wine for Es Cordelières since 1967. In this case, youthful ownership has brought energy, with the wines noted for their high quality. Wine has been made at Domaine Es Cordelières since at least the 15th century. It is across from Château Châtagneréaz, seen early on the hike. This second domain produces a Vaud Premier Grand Cru (Chasselas) and is part of the notable Clos, Domaines & Châteaux group. Terroir wines are a clear focus and the Graenichers are making the transition to biodynamic and organic production.

**Pinot Blanc pur:** Very long and slow pressing of the grapes and no second fermentation, resulting in a Pinot Blanc that has good tension and is unusually fresh and lively.

## ADDRESS

**Domaine de Penloup**
1180 Tartegnin
Tel: 079 671 7291
info@graenicher-vins.ch
graenicher-vins.ch

## WINERY FEES

There are various paid options, from wines with a snack to a meal and a walk in the vineyards plus a tasting session with the vigneron. Reserve ahead.

## WHERE ELSE TO FIND THIS CELLAR'S WINES NEARBY

**Hostellerie du Château**, Grand-Rue 16, 1180 Rolle,
021 822 32 62
info@lhotel-rolle.com
**Auberge Communale de la Clef d'Or**, Rte du Village 26, 1195 Bursinel,
021 824 11 06

# FÉCHY

## MEDIEVAL VILLAGE AND WORLD CHASSELAS CONSERVATORY

LA CÔTE

| ▷··· STARTING POINT | ···✗ DESTINATION |
|---|---|
| **AUBONNE GARE (BUS STATION)** | **DOMAINE LA COLOMBE, FÉCHY** |
| 📅 SEASON | HIKE TYPE |
| **YEAR-ROUND** | **EASY**  |
| ⌂ MAP REFERENCE | 🕐 DURATION |
| **SHEET 261T** | **2H 15M** |
| | ↦ LENGTH |
| 🔍 INTERESTING SIGHTS | **8.3 KM** |
| OLD TOWN OF AUBONNE. CHASSELAS WORLD CONSERVATORY. | ∿ CLIMB / DESCENT |
| | **165 M / 229 M** |

# BAYEL GRAND CRU
DOMAINE LA COLOMBE

WHITE

CITRUS,
SOME VINTAGES LINDEN/
LIME TREE

LIGHT AND AIRY,
BALANCED

DRY,
STILL

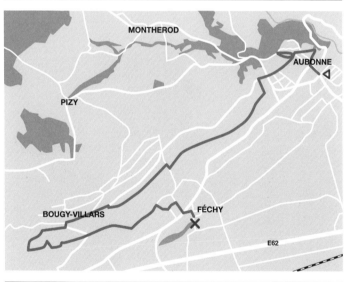

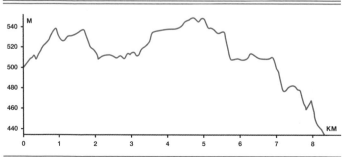

# DESCRIPTION OF THE ROUTE

From the bus station head uphill and into the center of the old town. Go uphill, jog to the right (Administration Communale building is on the left) and then to the left onto Rue des Marchands; from here simply make a loop to view the homes of the old bourgeoisie. The bustling little town at the foot of the 12th century defensive castle is worth a wander to admire the strength of medieval knees: steep streets and high, narrow attached houses.

The trail leaves the town at the intersection (a short block from Grande-Rue) of Rue des Fossés-Dessus and Rue du Chaffard, which becomes Route de Bougy after you cross the busy road that goes up to the Signal de Bougy park. One of Vaud's finest private castles, the 18th c. Bougy-Saint-Martin, sits on this corner. It's a reminder of the historic Swiss discretion surrounding money: today the fortune made from providing special inks for Swiss bank notes is linked to the castle.

Turn left at Sous-Bougy and head downhill until Chemin des Curzilles; turn right; it briefly fades to a track. Domaine La Colombe has markers for its terroir wines whose grapes come from specific vine parcels. The first

one is just after Aubonne, the famous En Curzille vines on the right. Several grape varieties grow together here, referred to as complanted vines. Vignerons often used the system in the past to reduce the risk of disease, but it's little used today because the grapes don't ripen at the same time.

Continue straight with two small jogs, right-left at the T-junction and the same at a second T-junction, Château de Riencourt, onto Chemin de la Plantaz, turn right, continue until you reach the Grande Rue of Bougy village. Bougy is a breezy single main street village along the ridge at the top of the vines. On a clear day you can see the 140-metre high Jet d'Eau, nearly 40 km away in Geneva. Keep straight through the village and stay on the main street as it bends left. Turn right at Chemin des Civières and stay on the road as it heads downhill.

Stop at the Chasselas World Conservatory panel, follow the footpath along the bottom of the rows of vines that are marked with the names of grape varieties. This is a remarkable research project, a collection of rare vines. The Chasselas World Conservatory and another in Lavaux were created to preserve all known varieties of this grape. Chasselas Fendant Roux is the grape used for the bulk of Chasselas wines, but the conservatory is home to oddball Chasselas grapes like Blanchette and Giclet, in the hope of safeguarding them to maintain diversity, needed to fight disease and the impact of climate change.

Retrace your path to Civières then take the first left to a small T-junction. Turn left to walk above the wooded area. Follow Chemin des Crosettes to the left and as it bends to the left until you cross Chemin de la Gaillarde onto Chemin du Mollard. Carry on straight until you reach a farm and junction; turn right and head downhill on Chemin du Chaummon. Continue until the road becomes Chemin des Barrettes at a small junction;

the Bayel (the selected wine) vineyard sign is on the right. This is also where the picturesque white Féchy church comes into view. The road becomes Chemin de Mi-Coteau; follow it as it bends right and heads into the village of Féchy and the church.

From the church head downhill on Chemin de la Crausaz, cross the busy main road onto Route du Saugey. Take a right turn at Route du Rionzier. The winery is just after the auberge.

**Return**
From the winery, 100 m to a bus stop. The Allaman train station is a 30-minute easy walk.

**Notes**
Double check for the street sign at Chemin des Civières, because there are three options here and it's easy to take the wrong one.

For a longer, more strenuous hike, a loop up to Signal de Bougy, the hugely popular park and golf driving range owned by the Migros coop-erative foundation turns this into an 11 km hike with an elevation gain / loss of 306 / 371. Via Les Cassivettes, La Bossenaz, Pizy, Signal de Bougy, Chemin du Signal.

# DOMAINE LA COLOMBE

Raymond Paccot is a pioneer of contemporary Swiss wines – precise, clean, discreet wines tied closely to their place of origin. He shifted to biodynamic wine production in the 2010s. Daughter Laura's mission to produce wines as naturally as possible follows his lead. Their Bayel is a classic, award-winning La Côte Chasselas. This eponymous grape, born in the region, is known for its delicate but wide register of notes. La Colombe has a Chasselas lineup from the terroirs seen on the hike, and tasting the range is a great introduction to the grape.

**Bayel Grand Cru:** low acidity, easy to drink, a classic high quality Chasselas from canton Vaud.

## ADDRESS

**Domaine La Colombe**
Route du Monastère 1
1173 Féchy
Tel: 021 808 6648
domaine@lacolombe.ch
lacolombe.ch

## WINERY FEES

CHF20/person
Refunded if you buy 6 bottles.

Chasselas World Conservatory
c/o La Colombe
https://www.conservatoiremondialduchasselas.com

## WHERE ELSE TO FIND THIS CELLAR'S WINES NEARBY

**Njørden**, Pl. du Marché 15, 1170 Aubonne,
021 808 50 90
contact@njorden.com
**Café du Port**, Rue du Port 9, 1180 Rolle,
021 825 15 20
info@nrt.ch
**Hostellerie du Château**, Grand-Rue 16, 1180 Rolle,
021 822 32 62
info@lhotel-rolle.com
**Auberge communale de Féchy**, Rte du Rionzier 3, 1173 Féchy,
021 808 03 35
info@aubergefechy.ch

# SAINT-PREX

INGENIOUS 17TH CENTURY ENGINEERING, OLD GRAPES, NEW GLASS

LA CÔTE

|  ▷⋯ STARTING POINT | ⋯✗ DESTINATION |
|---|---|
| **ETOY TRAIN STATION** | **DOMAINE DE TERRE-NEUVE, SAINT-PREX** |

|  SEASON |  HIKE TYPE |
|---|---|
| **YEAR-ROUND** | **EASY**  |

| MAP REFERENCE | DURATION |
|---|---|
| **SHEET 261T** | **1H 45M** |
| | ↦ LENGTH |
| | **6.8 KM** |

|  INTERESTING SIGHTS | ⤳ CLIMB / DESCENT |
|---|---|
| LAKESIDE WALK: EAST INTO ST. PREX. VIEUX BOURG. VILLAGE MANOR HOUSE. THE WAST. THE WAY OF ST. JAMES. | **74 M / 82 M** |

PINOT NOIR,
SERVAGNIN
VARIETY

# SERVAGNIN
# MORGES
## DOMAINE DE
## TERRE-NEUVE

 RED

 RICH BLACK CHERRY
FRUIT

RED BERRIES;
SMOOTH AND BALANCED
FROM SILKY TANNINS

 DRY,
STILL

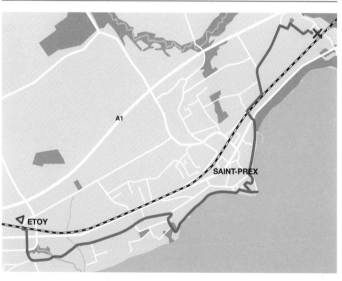

A1

SAINT-PREX

ETOY

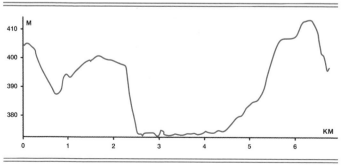

# DESCRIPTION OF THE ROUTE

The train station in Etoy deposits travellers on the edge of the industrial and commercial zone. Head straight downhill towards the lake, crossing the busy roundabout on the cantonal highway. At the T-junction after a second roundabout turn left onto the Buchillon to Saint-Prex road, shared with cyclists and the occasional car. Walk as far as signs for Coulet and the STEP (water treatment plant) and turn right, walking downhill on the Chemin de Coulet until you reach the small park and Coulet beach. This is the start of a sheltered waterfront walk developed a few years ago, a happy exception to the rule that private property owners along Lake Geneva prevent the public from having access to the waterfront.

Take time to explore the *Vieux Bourg*, or old town, once you reach Saint-Prex. It is a small triangular piece of land bordered on one side by a street called Pont Levis in memory of the moat that long ago separated the village from the rest of the world. In the 18th century,

engineers redeveloped the old town so that all streets curve slightly and are interrupted by cross streets, a ruse to keep at bay the wild winds that can blow off Lake Geneva. The center is remarkably calm on even the stormiest winter days.

At the primary school, right after a park that signals the end of the waterfront walk, turn left then take the first right. A 20-step detour to the Bains des Dames recalls an era when women had the privacy of their own small beach. Retrace, turn right and follow the street to the end past the *Manoir* and a fountain to reach the boat dock where lake steamers land. Backtrack to the Grand'Rue and walk towards the clock tower, turn right shortly before to follow one of the small, protected streets to the 12th century chateau with its square dungeon, a building that later served as a grain storehouse, and onto the lakefront park.

Follow Avenue de Taillecou nearly to the end, where it meets the cantonal highway. Turn left and cross the highway, taking the railway underpass along Chemin du Perreret and turn right immediately after, walking along the Chemin de Pomeiry. The road bends left at a bench and panel for the Way of St. James European hiking trail. Follow the road rather than the path parallel to the railroad tracks. It bends right as the Chemin de Bon Boccard, past farmhouses set back from the road. The trail takes a right before reaching the A1 autoroute and heads downhill behind Terre Neuve, with its vineyards and gracious park of grounds with old trees.

## Return
Ten-minute walk back to Saint-Prex on a path next to the track to a lakefront bus stop.

## Notes
Saint-Prex is rich in history, from the stilt-houses of early settlers to its role in Roman expansion and, later, three centuries as a summer holiday break from Morges, to its reincarnation as a glass-making town (sandy beaches as raw material) and then, in the 20th century, glass recycling center, one of three in Switzerland, a nation that recycles 95% or more of its glass, mostly for wine bottles. It's a five-minute detour from the lakefront park uphill towards the train station to the 12th century Roman church.

# DOMAINE DE TERRE-NEUVE

Wine has been made here for 200 years, as witnessed by the ancient cedars, lime trees and oaks in the winery's large park. David Kind has been making wines here since 1996; his son, who worked with him for 10 years, now has a nearby cellar. The wine is of a very high quality and the winery itself remains a quiet, peaceful haven despite sitting between highways and a main rail line.

 **Servagnin Morges:** This is a wine designed to reflect history. Servagnin was the first Pinot Noir grown in Switzerland, but by the late 20th century it was nearly extinct, the victim of more productive versions of the grape. It was saved *in extremis* by a handful of vignerons. Servagnin today is made only from grapes grown in the Morges wine area, from the variety of that name. The wine must meet standards that are checked: grapes must be fully ripened, the yields in the vineyard must be very low and the wine matured in oak barrels for 16 months. The first vines came to St-Prex via Marie de Bourgogne, the daughter of Philip the Bold, Duke of Burgundy. He famously banned Gamay from the vineyards of Burgundy's Côte d'Or in 1395 because of his love for Pinot Noir. His daughter fled from the plague in Morges to the safety of St-Prex while pregnant with her 10th child. She thanked the villagers by offering them the vines she and her father loved.

## ADDRESS

**Domaine de Terre-Neuve**
1162 Saint-Prex, Vaud
Tel: 079 216 94 44
info@terreneuve.ch
terreneuve.ch

## WINERY FEES

No.
Regular hours; call ahead.

## WHERE ELSE TO FIND THIS CELLAR'S WINES NEARBY

**Restaurant Le Taillecou**, Av. de Taillecou 4, 1162 Saint-Prex,
021 806 11 98
**Auberge de l'Union**, Rue du Pont-Levis 11, 1162 Saint-Prex,
021 544 35 77
info@auberge-union.com
**La Croix Fédérale**, Rue du Pont-Levis 10, 1162 Saint-Prex,
021 806 10 28

# ÉCHICHENS

## SHHHH, RIVERSIDE VAUD: FISH AT PLAY, BEES AT WORK

LA CÔTE

| ▷··· STARTING POINT | ···✕ DESTINATION |
|---|---|
| **SAINT-PREX, LAKEFRONT PARK PLACE D'ARMES** | **DOMAINE HENRI CRUCHON, ÉCHICHENS** |

 SEASON |  HIKE TYPE

**YEAR-ROUND** | **MODERATE**

 MAP REFERENCE | ⏱ DURATION

**SHEET 261T** | **3H**

| | ↦ LENGTH |

🔍 INTERESTING SIGHTS | **11.7 KM**

ST. PREX AND MORGES LAKEFRONT PARKS.
LE BOIRON HIDDEN RIVER.
CASTLE WITH MILITARY/ARTILLERY HISTORY
MUSEUM | ∿ CLIMB / DESCENT

| | **229 M / 138 M** |

# PINOT NOIR GRAND CRU CHAMPANEL
## DOMAINE HENRI CRUCHON

RED

FRUITY WITH A HINT OF VEGETABLES – DISTINCTIVE CHARACTER

ELEGANT AND CLASSY WHILE ALSO POWERFUL, AND YET PINOT NOIR SMOOTHNESS

DRY, STILL

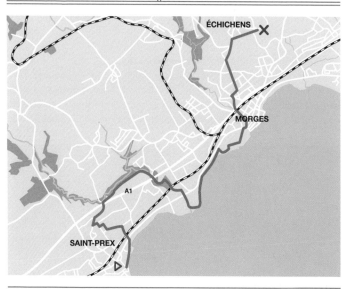

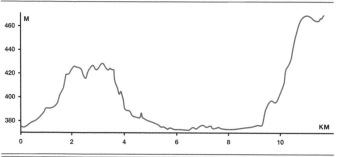

# DESCRIPTION OF THE ROUTE

The lakefront park in Saint-Prex is an easy five-minute walk from the train station, a regular stop on the regional line. The park is crowded with local families on sunny summer days but is otherwise calm. Walk along the village waterfront in the direction of Morges and the view includes the small, typical Lake Geneva village pleasure boat port, scores of kite-surfers (if it's a windy day), hilly Lausanne gleaming white in the distance and, across the lake, Evian, France. Cross at the busy main road, then pass under the train line and keep straight to the T-junction where you turn left to walk alongside the communal garden plots. At the school take a right turn then jog left and right (alternatively, if you spot it, follow a short signposted footpath to the top of the hill).

The autoroute is to the left and Perceval Educational Center to the right as the Route de Lussy takes you out of town; cross under the highway and a few meters later leave the road at the sign for Le Sentier de la Truite, an educational trail with panels that explain the migration of local river fish. The trail here skirts the edge of a heavily wooded area, but there is a second parallel footpath that leads into the forest and down to the river, following the Sentier de la Truite. Note that the forest trail is not always clearly marked.

At a small intersection where the road to the right leads to a nearby farm, take the sharp left turn, head downhill and into the woods on a small local road. The trail joins the Boiron River woodlands path immediately before the STEP, or water recycling plant. It is easy to miss: take the small blacktop path and look for a yellow diamond on

an overgrown tree. This is a beautiful wooded trail, peaceful despite passing under the autoroute at one point, with the walk closely following the shallow, winding Boiron, a river that is mostly hidden from view unless you're hiking the trail. Continue through the woods until a beekeeper's hut – there's a bee warning sign for hikers! – at which point the trail moves into open ground, alongside Tolochenaz farms with small markets.

From this point until you arrive at Independence Park in Morges, the trail is a river and shoreline walk – occasionally on sand – that is well sign-posted and easy to follow, with an excellent set of educational panels about rivers that feed into Lake Geneva. Walk along the Boiron's final stages until it feeds into the lake, past a water research center and fishermen's small docks on this protected inlet, then one of the nicest quiet stretches of this lake, where water laps gently next to the trail. Morges has an impressive lakefront park area with first a collection of swimming pools, then Independence Park with one of Europe's largest and finest tulip displays every April and May. It sits next to the Morges Castle, built by Louis de Savoie in the 13th century to protect the city. Today the castle houses five museums, including military and artillery history museums.

From here the trail cuts through the center of this regionally important commercial town and up to the Morges train station, where the trail veers right at the roundabout above the station before heading more steeply uphill through a residential area. Alternatively you can continue on Avenue de Marcelin, but it is a busy road. You suddenly come to a startling spread of vineyards and to the left Marcelin, which is canton Vaud's post-secondary vineyard and winemaking school. The road soon rejoins Avenue de Marcelin, quieter at this point. Continue uphill, now in the countryside, until you reach a small road signposted for Echichens; turn right and walk to the winery.

**Return**

Domaine Henri Cruchon is just above the Morges hospital (five minute walk), which has good bus service to the train station.

**Notes**

Wine: The Cruchons offer the rare chance to compare biodynamic and classic wines from the same winery, with information about how they decide which method to use for particular vine parcels and grapes.

Hiking: A small and worthwhile trail detour, especially in mid-summer: walk from Morges Castle past the boat harbor and along the quay, famous for its display of dahlias from June to late summer. Loop back along the parallel Rue Louis de Savoie to enjoy typical 17th to 19th century Vaud town architecture, then rejoin the trail next to the castle.

# DOMAINE HENRI CRUCHON

This is a relatively large family winery by Swiss standards, with several members of different generations actively involved and a broad range of well-respected wines. They were early converts to biodynamic working methods and with time and experience they have gained considerable expertise, which they share generously. Seventeen grape varieties are grown on their mosaic of vine parcels throughout the region, with the emphasis placed on understanding how the terroir of these varied vineyard patches works with a mix of grapes. Champanel is a vine parcel on the right side of the road as you head down from the winery to Morges hospital. A Chasselas white as well as this red are made from its grapes. Both are wines with distinctive characters.

**Pinot Noir Grand Cru Champanel:** great character, a wine to have with creamy cheeses and flavourful meats.

## ADDRESS

**Henri Cruchon**
Route du Village 32
1112 Échichens
Tel: 021 801 17 92
contact@henricruchon.com
henricruchon.com

## WINERY FEES

CHF15/person and an option for tasting with a cheese platter, fee refunded if you buy six bottles.
Weekdays 10–6, closed 12–2
Saturdays 8–12

## WHERE ELSE TO FIND THIS CELLAR'S WINES NEARBY

**Romantik Hôtel Mont-Blanc Au Lac**, Rue des Alpes 1, 1110 Morges, 021 804 87 87
info@hotel-mont-blanc.ch

# VALEYRES

## ANCIENT ABBEY NESTLED IN HILLS AND DREAMY GORGES

CÔTES DE L'ORBE

| ▷⋯ STARTING POINT | ⋯✗ DESTINATION |
|---|---|
| **ROMAINMÔTIER HILLTOP MAIN BUS STOP** | **CHÂTEAU DE VALEYRES, VALEYRES-SOUS-RANCES** |

 SEASON

**YEAR-ROUND**

 HIKE TYPE

**MODERATE**

 MAP REFERENCE

**SHEET 251T**

⊙ DURATION

**3H 30M**

↦ LENGTH

**13 KM**

 INTERESTING SIGHTS

ROMAINMÔTIER ABBEY.
ORBE RIVER. VALEYRES CASTLE.

〜 CLIMB / DESCENT

**310 M / 476 M**

# LE COURSON
## CHÂTEAU DE VALEYRES

 RED

 RIPE FRUITS,
PLUM AND RED BERRIES

 VELVETY, WELL-STRUCTURED
— AN EXCELLENT EXAMPLE
OF THESE GRAPES

 DRY,
STILL

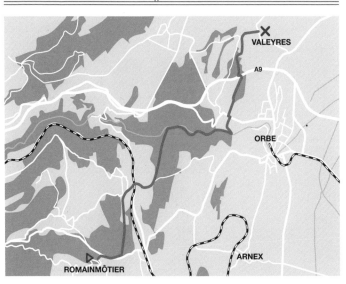

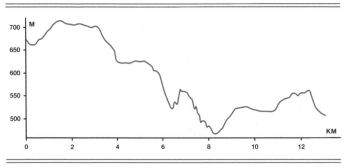

# DESCRIPTION OF THE ROUTE

From the main bus stop at the top of the hill, head down towards the abbey, clearly visible, and take time to wander around the small streets. Return to the starting point to pick up a popular footpath (great for dog-walking) that initially runs parallel to the road. After a few minutes the trail turns left, before Croy. Continue straight on this path through the Forel woods, along a small ridge above the village of Croy.

At the entrance to Bretonnières the trail joins the road into town; turn right. The road becomes Rue Etienne, bending right; stay on this as it crosses the A9 autoroute. This is the road to Agiez, but shortly after the A9 take the footpath shortcut that avoids a loop in the road (the road is visible).

The trail briefly shares the road then veers left (look for the yellow trail arrows) along a footpath at the edge of woods. It runs roughly parallel to a small river as it heads north. When it jogs slightly right to go further into the woods, be sure to stay on the marked footpath (a couple of farm buildings should be on the left).

Where the trail splits, the right path goes towards Agiez; stay left, following signs for the Gorges de l'Orbe. Continue straight on the trail, through the woods, to the Orbes River – at this point the trail merges with part of the beautiful 17 km Vallorbe-Orbe trail called the Gorges de l'Orbe. The signs can be confusing because an older, riverside trail was improved in 2020 when a higher and somewhat safer trail was created; both are in service and can be used. Follow the trail as it bends right, keeping the river on the left. Continue until the bridge. At the hydro-electric power station on the other side of the river – pylons and overhead wires just before are a clue.

The trail leaves the woods and riverbanks at this point. Head slightly uphill on a small road with big loops, then straight, with the power plant on the left. The trail very briefly joins the road into Montcherand but quickly turns right to continue north towards Valeyres-sous-Rances, alongside fields and small woods. It crosses the A9 autoroute and the trail splits: take the lefthand option, a small road, and soon after, when the road becomes a footpath and bends right, follow it through light woods and a bit later next to fields on the right, into the village. Just before the village go left and then right to go around a cemetery, then follow the street to Chemin du Moty and straight to a junction where it joins Rue du Village. At the main intersection turn right and the winery is on the right, in the castle courtyard.

**Return**
Bus stop outside the winery.

**Notes**
Romainmôtier is a popular tourist attraction, in part because of its charming hilly streets and medieval charm, but mainly for its 11th century Cluniac Abbey and beautiful stained glass windows. The trail takes a brief detour down into the village from the hilltop bus stop, but this is a place where hikers might want to allow more time.

Hiking in winter is not a problem unless there's been a recent large snowfall, but beware that this is the season for thinning the forests and woodcutters (always signposted) abound!

Another detour that is a popular tourist destination is 1.5 km off the trail, but an easy hike: Roman mosaic tiles in an archaeological setting, a small outpost next to the autoroute on the edge of Orbe. Note it is open April–October.

# CHÂTEAU DE VALEYRES

The 17th century chateau is Bernese style, reflecting the important role its owners and others from Bern played in the history of this northern tip of canton Vaud. Benjamin Morel and his siblings are the third generation; the family bought the chateau in 2004 and recently began renovations. The winery is in a part of canton Vaud whose good wine reputation suffered for some years despite this being the oldest Swiss vineyard area. Benjamin Morel and a close colleague, Frédéric Hostettler, have been leading a renaissance of regional wines and the results are gaining national attention. They are working closely with a handful of other local producers to raise the profile of Côtes de l'Orbe wines.

**Le Courson:** This is one of the winery's early wines. It gained considerable attention as a success story for these grapes, which were created by the Swiss agricultural research station some 50 years ago. The winery has built on this reputation for blending, not traditionally a Swiss winemaking strength.

## ADDRESS

**Château de Valeyres**
Rue du Village 5
1358 Valeyres-sous-Rances
Tel: 079 658 2614
info@chateauvaleyres.ch
chateauvaleyres.ch

## WINERY FEES

No.
Open Saturday mornings and by appointment.

## WHERE ELSE TO FIND THIS CELLAR'S WINES NEARBY

**Restaurant A La Vieille Auberge**, Rte Romaine 2,
1358 Valeyres-sous-Rances,
024 441 00 06

# ARAN-VILLETTE

## EMBLEMATIC "THREE SUNS" LAVAUX TERRACED VINES

LAVAUX

---

| ▷··· STARTING POINT | ···✗ DESTINATION |
|---|---|
| **CHEXBRES TRAIN STATION** | **DOMAINE MERMETUS, ARAN (BOURG-EN-LAVAUX)** |

 SEASON

**YEAR-ROUND**

 HIKE TYPE

**MODERATE**

 MAP REFERENCE

**SHEET 261T**

🕐 DURATION

**2H 15M**

↦ LENGTH

**8.2 KM**

 INTERESTING SIGHTS

LAVAUX'S UNESCO WORLD HERITAGE SITE VINEYARDS. DÉZALEY STONE WALL AND CASTLES. LAKE GENEVA VIEWS.

〰 CLIMB / DESCENT

**307 M / 269 M**

GAMAY,
OLD
VARIETY

# PLANT ROBERT
## DOMAINE MERMETUS

RED

SPICY,
BLACK PEPPER,
STRAWBERRIES

DEEPER AND MORE
MOUTH-FILLING THAN
CONTEMPORARY CLONE
GAMAYS

DRY,
STILL

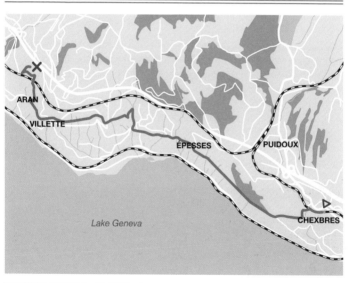

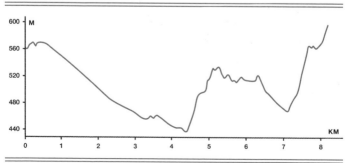

# DESCRIPTION OF THE ROUTE

From the S7 train station in Chexbres, head west then downhill at the edge of Chexbres village, past an old mill, until you join the Corniche road. This is a kind of shelf that meanders above the lake with fine views of the vines and lake below. Walk to the village of Epesses and along the top end, heading in the direction of Riex. Shortly before Epesses you see the large "Dézaley" sign on the rock face. This is Lavaux winery country par excellence, with Chasselas making up 90% of the grapes, grown in a variety of soils. Dézaley is the oldest cultivated vine parcel in the UNESCO-listed Lavaux vineyards and nearby is the Middle Ages Tour de Marsens.

Not long ago, vignerons in these villages opted to move completely to organic production and you'll see many signs designed to educate the public about flora, fauna, and sustainable winemaking.

In Riex, at the roundabout as you exit the village, the trail goes uphill along a steep little road with a stream to the right, vineyards to the left – and a fine picnic spot at the top of the hill, just as the trail turns left to head along another more private shelf road.

The trail takes you through several quiet little hamlets where winemaking remains at the center of everything. When you come to Aran, a village with some fine old buildings, including the church. Here, look for footpath signs (a bit to the right of the church) that will take you uphill. The narrow farm road from Aran to Mermetus is dauntingly steep, but little used and the views are wonderful. Cross under the train tracks and turn left, walk along a small road through vineyards that include some very special grapes grown by Mermetus, then take a sharp right and continue uphill. The winery is on the right before the autoroute.

**Return**

From the winery, walk uphill (allow 10 minutes) and under the autoroute, then turn left to the no. 67 bus stop, which goes to the Cully train station on the Vevey-Lausanne line.

**Notes**

The "three suns" describes the process of the vines first being warmed by the sun in the sky, the heat retained by the walls, and the mirror effects of the lake.

The final uphill trek is very steep. The view from the garden is worth it, as is the warm family welcome.

# DOMAINE MERMETUS

This is one of the highest Lavaux wineries, next to the A9 autoroute, a point where altitude and soil differences give the Chollet family wines a distinctive character. Remarkably, they have some 100-year-old vines. They also have some of the most charming wine labels and corks around! Papa Henri worked as a graphic designer when young, and his whimsical designs are a hallmark of the winery. Plant Robert is not their signature wine, as it is not always available, but it has done much to make their reputation. They were one of the saviors of this old and now rare variety of Gamay with a colourful past (ask about the robbers). For Plant Robert lovers, this winery makes one of the best, a wine that is deep and spicy on the palate.

**Plant Robert:** Flavourful and easy to drink, with a wonderful story about saving the grape *in extremis*.

## ADDRESS

**Domaine Mermetus**
Chemin du Graboz 2
1091 Aran-Villette
Tel: 021 799 24 85
info@mermetus.ch
mermetus.ch

## WINERY FEES

No. By appointment.

## WHERE ELSE TO FIND THIS CELLAR'S WINES NEARBY

**Lavaux Vinorama**, Rte du Lac 2, 1071 Rivaz,
021 946 31 31
info@lavaux-vinorama.ch

# CULLY

## LAKESIDE WORLD HERITAGE VINEYARDS RAMBLE

LAVAUX

| ▷⋯ STARTING POINT | ⋯✕ DESTINATION |
|---|---|
| **VEVEY TRAIN STATION** | **DOMAINE LOUIS BOVARD, CULLY** |

 SEASON |  HIKE TYPE

**YEAR-ROUND** | **EASY**

 MAP REFERENCE | ⏱ DURATION

**SHEET 261T** | **3H 10M**

| ↦ LENGTH |
| **12.8 KM** |

🔍 INTERESTING SIGHTS

NESTLÉ WORLD HEADQUARTERS.
CHARLIE CHAPLIN'S GRAVE.
LAVAUX VINEYARDS. ST. SAPHORIN.
JAZZ VILLAGE OF CULLY.

〰 CLIMB / DESCENT

**361 M / 369 M**

# MÉDINETTE
## DOMAINE LOUIS BOVARD

 WHITE

 TOAST,
FLINT,
DRIED FRUITS

 REMARKABLE MINERALITY

 DRY,
STILL

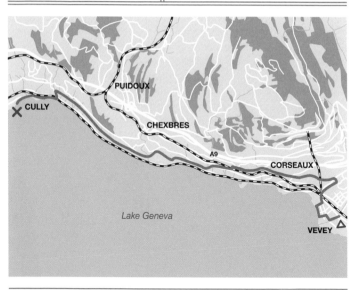

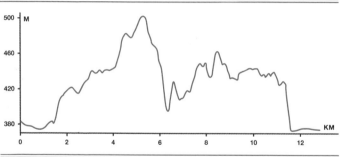

# DESCRIPTION OF THE ROUTE

Walk from the station down to and through old Vevey and briefly along the waterfront. Turn to the right at Nestlé's world headquarters and head towards the hillside. After crossing the busy main road you will see the funicular that goes up to Mount Pèlerin; stay on the right side of the road and follow signs for Charlie Chaplin's grave. The peaceful little well-shaded cemetery is a two-minute walk from the road and a stone's throw from the home where the filmmaker/actor and his large family lived.

Retrace steps to the main road, cross over and follow Route du Cyprès through a residential area – keep eyes out for the roadside neolithic tomb! – to the center of Corseaux. Stay left at the Y-junction, continuing on Avenue des Jordils, then Avenue Félix-Cornu. At a Y-junction with Chemin de la Fin, turn right up this street and walk to the end, then turn left onto Chemin des Combes. At the T-junction go left onto Chemin de Chavonchin and continue some distance until an intersection with winery Henri Pinget on the left. Turn left and head down; the road bends right. Continue straight until Domaine du Burignon on the left: this is a magnificent old building, a hotel and winery owned by the city of Lausanne with vineyards dating back to the time of the Cistercian monks. Cross an often-busy Route de Vevey and from here it is a short and delightful, if steep, walk down to the

village of St. Saphorin. Allow some time to explore this jewel of a lakefront village that was once a fortified village, as its towers, arches, vaults and old stone buildings attest.

Heading northwest out of the village, parallel to the lake, take the left trail where it splits and follow signs to Rivaz. Enter the top end of the village and walk through to the lower end. Follow signs from here to Les Abbayes (an ancient winery owned by the city of Lausanne), Treytor-rens and Epesses, along the lowest road that runs parallel to the lake.

Epesses has an upper and lower part; stay below the main village, turning left at a collection of buildings and follow signs down to the train station. Here, cross under the railroad to pick up the lakefront path that leads to Cully, where the winery is in the center of the village on the lower end.

**Return**
Cully train station.

**Notes**

Around Dézaley this hike goes along some of the same trails as the Chexbres Epesses Aran Mermetus hike; there are several parallel paths in this area and you can generally swap to walk higher on the hillside or lower, for short distances. A map in this case will be very useful to avoid dead-ends.

Note that a major years-long project to renovate the lakefront is underway between Rivaz and Epesses, which at times will make it difficult to hike along the waterfront. The steep terraced hillside is slowly but inevitably sliding down towards the lake and the project aims to shore up the areas most at risk.

# DOMAINE LOUIS BOVARD

Louis Bovard, rarely seen without his captain's hat, is something of a legend in the world of Swiss wine; he was named an Icon of Swiss Wine by the *Gault&Millau guide* in 2016. He is a founder member of several influential groups including the Mémoire des Vins Suisses, the Barony of Dézaley and Arte Vitis. He is the man behind the creation of the Conservatoire Mondial du Chasselas, which researches older grape clonal selections. And he was a pioneer of using oak with Chasselas, rarely done but a key feature of aging these wines from terroirs that produce grapes capable of it, notably Dézaley.

 **Médinette:** This is a classic wine, one of the earliest modern commercial successes for Chasselas, well-known and loved throughout Switzerland. While it is generally drunk young, it is famous for its ability to age very well, from 20–40 years. It is equally famous for its label, described by the winemaker: "It represents the Bacchus of the 1905 Winegrowers' Festival, a role played by a nephew of the family, Albert Bovard, who is shown here without his mythical leopard-skin outfit. The name Médinette refers to the city of Medinet-Habu, located near Thebes in Upper Egypt, one of whose temples is dedicated to the work and divinities of the vine and wine."

## ADDRESS

**Domaine Louis Bovard**
Place d'armes, 2
1096 Cully, Vaud
Tel: 021 799 2125
vin@domainebovard.com
domainebovard.com

## WINERY FEES

No
Open M–F, 8:30–12:00 and 14:00–17:00

## WHERE ELSE TO FIND THIS CELLAR'S WINES NEARBY

**Vinothèque La Maison Rose**, Pl. d'Armes 6, 1096 Cully,
021 799 55 66
vin@domainebovard.com
**Café de Riex**, Rte de la Corniche 24, 1097 Riex,
021 799 13 06
**Le Major Davel**, Pl. d'Armes 8, 1096 Cully,
021 552 19 50
info@major-davel.ch
**Tout un Monde**, Pl. du Village 7, 1091 Grandvaux,
021 799 14 14
info@toutunmonde.ch

# VILLENEUVE

## WHERE THE RHONE FEEDS LAKE GENEVA, ANCIENT LAKE NAVIGATION

CHABLAIS

| ▷⋯ STARTING POINT | ⋯✗ DESTINATION |
|---|---|
| **SAINT-GINGOLPH GARE (TRAIN STATION)** | **CAVE DES ROIS, VILLENEUVE** |

|  SEASON | HIKE TYPE |
|---|---|
| **YEAR-ROUND** | **EASY**  |

| MAP REFERENCE | ◷ DURATION |
|---|---|
| **SHEET 262T** | **3H 30M** |
| | ↦ LENGTH |
| | **13.6 KM** |
| ⌕ INTERESTING SIGHTS | ⌇ CLIMB / DESCENT |
|  ST. GINGOLPH'S LAKE BARGES MUSEUM. BOUVERET (RHONE MEETS LAKE GENEVA). STEAM TRAIN PARK. | **264 M / 113 M** |

## SYRAH LES EVOUETTES
### CAVE DES ROIS

RED

SPICES,
A HINT OF GREEN PEPPER

RICH,
ROUND,
SMOOTH

OAKED,
MATURED IN BARRELS,
NEW OAK

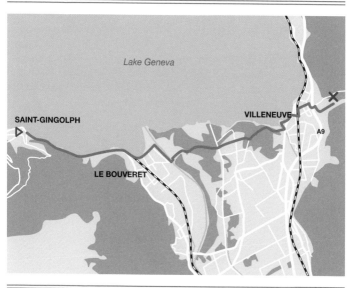

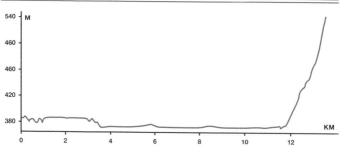

# DESCRIPTION OF THE ROUTE

St. Gingolph, to the surprise of many, is part of Canton Valais despite sitting on the edge of Lake Geneva, which is mostly bordered by Vaud and Geneva. The town is the end of the Swiss train line around the lake on the French border. From the train station follow the road east towards the end of the lake. For those who are familiar with the view from the far busier side that is home to Montreux, Vevey and the A9 autoroute (which funnels skiers and hikers into canton Valais), this small, quiet village rich in history comes as a surprise. For centuries, it was a key lake navigation center ferrying stone, raw or wood products and chalk from the town and, from the other side of the lake, notably the market in Vevey, returning laden with wine, nuts, poultry, fruit and hay. The *cochères*, as the boats were known, shuttled between Evian, Geneva, Lausanne and Vevey until the early 20th century.

The trail follows a sidewalk along the border road to Bouveret, skipping a lovely but more challenging route up through the woods in order to enjoy wonderful views of the Lavaux UNESCO World Heritage site across the water. At Le Bout de la Forêt, a seminary, take the small road downhill to start walking along the waterfront; the entrance to Bouveret has a park with a playground and picnic area and occasional outdoor art exhibits.

Le Bouveret has two popular culture claims to fame, as the place where the Rhone River feeds into Lake Geneva, which is where the major Bol d'Or sailing race turns and heads back to Geneva, and as home to the Swiss Vapeur Parc, a ¼ scale steam train park.

One enters the waterfront area at the port, home to pleasure craft and fishing boats, with a dock for CGN lake boats. The walkway is lined with scores of small restaurants. The steam train park sits between the Stockalper Canal and the Rhone. It is home to 2 km of tracks with

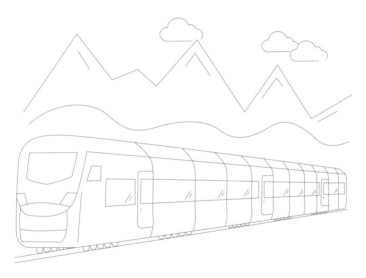

11 small coal-fired steam locomotives that loop around a small, idealized Switzerland of much greenery, 6 tunnels and 12 bridges – the park is popular for rides on the trains, but also for family walks.

The best places for seeing where the Rhone enters the lake are near the beach, on the left bank of the river, or follow a marked footpath upstream to the Passerelle des Grangettes, which crosses the Rhone. With the lake in view, about 300 metres away: head off the trail briefly, going downstream along the right bank on a footpath, before retracing steps to join the trail again. The trail crosses the Grand Canal, moves inland slightly until another canal at the start of Villeneuve. Here the trail picks up the shoreline again, offering views back towards St. Gingolph. At the CGN dock, turn right and start uphill, past the train station, crossing the busy main road and going over the A9 autoroute.

The walk up to Cave Les Rois is steep but the reward is a fine view of both the lake and Evouettes, where the land rises abruptly from the river to the Alps. The small patch of vineyards near the Rhone, is where the selected wine is grown.

**Return**
Walk back downhill and over the autoroute to the train station; allow 20 minutes.

**Notes**
The road from St. Gingolph becomes quite busy and noisy thanks to trucks and cross-border workers at rush hour, whereas it's relatively quiet most of the day.

An option is to walk part of the Chemin des Hameaux just above the winery; follow the signposts near a footbridge which is a few hundred metres up the Route de Plancudrey. Cross the bridge, then wander along paths that lead through forests and up to fine views.

# CAVE DES ROIS

Marco Grognuz is a longtime expert on Chasselas and member of the Terravin label commission which annually selects the best Vaud Chasselas after a series of high-level tastings throughout the year. His family winery is relatively large and they produce numerous wines from a dozen grape varieties, with vineyards in both Vaud and Valais, nearby Evouettes and Fully, upstream at the elbow of the Rhone.

**Syrah Les Evouettes:** while it can age, this is a Syrah that is designed for pleasure when drunk young.

## ADDRESS

**Cave des Rois**
Chez-les-Rois 2
1844 Villeneuve
Tel: 021 960 2038
Mobile: 076 370 7018
info@cavedesrois.ch
cavedesrois.ch

## WINERY FEES

No

## WHERE ELSE TO FIND THIS CELLAR'S WINES NEARBY

The winery has a second small tasting room in the center of Montreux.
**La Gondola Veneziana**, Grand Rue 89, 1844 Villeneuve,
021 960 31 36
sabine.spicher@hotmail.com

# OLLON

## GEOGRAPHY AND HISTORY, WHERE VAUD AND VALAIS MEET

CHABLAIS

| ▷··· STARTING POINT | ···✕ DESTINATION |
|---|---|
| **YVORNE, CLOS DE L'OMBRON** | **BERNARD CAVÉ VINS, OLLON** |

| 🗓 SEASON | 🗓 HIKE TYPE |
|---|---|
| **YEAR-ROUND** BUT SEE NOTE BELOW RE: SNOW | **MODERATE** 🚶 |

| ⛰ MAP REFERENCE | 🕐 DURATION |
|---|---|
| **SHEET 272T** | **3H** |
| | ↦ LENGTH |
| | **9.8 KM** |

| 🔍 INTERESTING SIGHTS | |
|---|---|
| YVORNE LANDSLIDE VINEYARDS. MAISON BLANCHE. AIGLE CASTLE. HIDDEN VINEYARDS OF OLLON. | 〽 CLIMB / DESCENT |
| | **416 M / 409 M** |

# GAMARET
## BERNARD CAVÉ VINS

RED

WOODLAND FRUITS,
BLACKBERRIES,
SOMEWHAT SUBTLE

SURPRISINGLY BIG: GOOD
STRUCTURE, SPICY,
RED BERRY FRUIT

DRY,
STILL

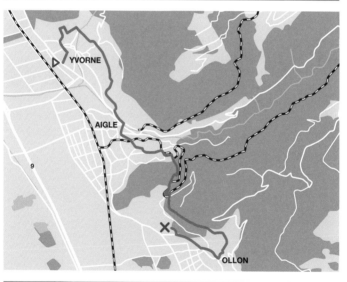

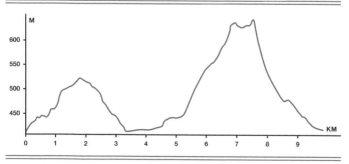

# DESCRIPTION OF THE ROUTE

From the bus stop on the main road in Yvorne head uphill and left: take in the broad view of the hillside, the notable site of a historical event. In 1584 a major landslide (known as the Ovaille) wiped out the village, leaving in its wake alluvial soil and gravel, a mix that is now famous for providing one of the best terroirs in the world for Chasselas wines. Walk up to the Maison Blanche following small roads through the vineyards, turning right at a collection of houses. The original manor house was built not long before the landslide, and the current white house with a tower, a landmark visible from afar, was built 25 years later, in 1609. Turn right at the top end of the house and follow the path across a stream, continuing straight through the hamlet of Vers Morey above the village of Yvorne (worth a detour). The trail carries on through the vineyards, where signs point to some of the biggest names in Vaud winemaking. Once past the top end of Yvorne the trail begins to head downhill towards La Grande Eau, a tributary of the Rhone.

Follow the river briefly, then cross over the second narrow bridge, coming out at a roundabout with schools on the left. Carry on straight, around the edge of Aigle's town centre to the narrow streets in the charming bourg of Le Cloître at the foot of the Aigle castle. Turn left to walk up to the castle; the trail leads through the courtyard, which houses the interactive Musée de la Vigne et du Vin. The trail bends left to take you around the back side of the castle, with fine views of this 12th century chateau and its vineyards. The castle was built by the

Chevaliers d'Aigle, destroyed by the Bern Republic when it attacked the region, and was rebuilt by the Bernese to house their governors. In 1970 was renovated to house the museum and event rooms.

Follow yellow walking path signs to the right at the first junction. Continue straight, heading uphill towards the woods and bluffs. The trail leads to the hamlet of Verschiez, climbing gently through the woods. Do not stray from the trail here – the bluffs fall abruptly to the valley floor! Shortly before Verschiez the trail cuts sharply to the left; in snowy weather use the option to continue straight towards the houses and use the small road until it rejoins the trail.

The trail continues pleasantly through the Bois de Glaive until you suddenly come to open fields and vines, with views to the southeast – the peaks of canton Valais are visible. This is one part of Ollon's vineyards, hidden from most views. The trail leads you downhill and into the village. Turn right at the Place de l'Hotel de Ville to stay in the village and above the often busy Route d'Aigle for as long as possible. Shortly after the train station, as you head downhill, stay on the left side of the road and join the parallel smaller road, Chemin des Truits. Then go along the small footpath between Chemin des Truits and the Route d'Aigle until there is an opportunity to cross the road (there is a vineyard on the opposite side). Follow the footpath on this side of the road until it ends, then walk for another 50 metres to the start of the long driveway to the winery, which is set back from the road on the right, easily visible.

**Return**

The Ollon train station or bus service from St. Triphon village, on foot (14–15 minutes).

**Notes**

The trail is fine all year unless there is heavy snow down to the plain. In this case, the highest part of the walk, above Ollon, becomes difficult. An alternative: at the point where the trail takes a sharp left bend and climbs up through the forest, follow the road to the right to the small collection of houses called Verschiez. The parallel road from Verschiez is lower than the trail and accessible to car traffic, so it tends to be clear.

# BERNARD CAVÉ VINS

Bernard Cavé is one of the busiest and most respected oenologists in the region, overseeing wine production and counselling a number of other cellars to develop their lines of wines. He started out working for a wine merchant, studied winemaking, then opened a consulting business in 1995, in addition to making 4,000 litres of wine under his own name. Today he makes some 200,000 litres – and another 300,000 for other wineries, working with 33 grape varieties in an area that covers roughly the three villages on this trail. The Gamaret is from a vineyard on the far side of Ollon, close to the Bex Salt Mines in Antagnes.

**Gamaret:** Gamaret is a contemporary grape cross (Gamay Noir x Reichensteiner) created in Switzerland, released in 1990, with strong resistance to some diseases. It's often used in blends to add tannins, colour, power. It is increasingly made as a single grape wine with Bernard Cavé as one of the earliest to develop this. The second fermentation is in barrels and the wine then matures in oak.

## ADDRESS

**Bernard Cavé Vins**
En Chatoney
1867 Ollon (VD)
Tel: 024 499 2958
Mobile 079 210 7416
bernard.cave@bluewin.ch
bernardcavevins.ch

## WINERY FEES

No

## WHERE ELSE TO FIND THIS CELLAR'S WINES NEARBY

**Auberge du Bouillet**, Rte des Mines de Sel 50, 1880 Bex,
024 463 27 72

# VALAIS

# MARTIGNY-COMBE

## GOLDEN TRIANGLE, DRAMATIC TERRACES, RHONE RIVER

LOWER VALAIS

| ▷⋯ STARTING POINT | ⋯✗ DESTINATION |
|---|---|
| MARTIGNY CROIX, CROISÉE: MULTIPLE LINES BUS STOP | DOMAINE GÉRALD BESSE, MARTIGNY-CROIX |

| 🗓 SEASON | 🎛 HIKE TYPE |
|---|---|
| YEAR-ROUND | MODERATE 🚶 |

| ⛰ MAP REFERENCE | ⏱ DURATION |
|---|---|
| SHEET 282T | 2H 45M |

| | ↦ LENGTH |
|---|---|
| | 7.4 KM |

| 🔍 INTERESTING SIGHTS | ∿ CLIMB / DESCENT |
|---|---|
| PLAN CÉRISIER. VIEW OF UPPER RHONE. DRYSTONE VINEYARD WALLS. CHATEAU RUINS. TERRACED VINEYARDS. | 561 M / 435 M |

# GAMAY
# ST. THÉODULE
### GÉRALD BESSE WINERY

RED

BLACK FRUITS,
SPICES,
VIOLETS

SMOOTH AND ELEGANT,
GOOD STRUCTURE WITH
FIRM TANNINS

DRY,
STILL

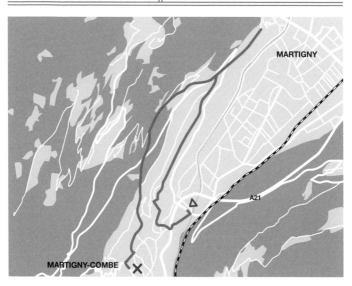

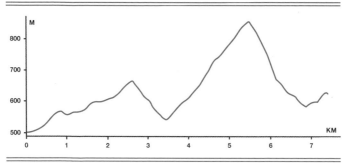

# DESCRIPTION OF THE ROUTE

From the Martigny Croix, Croisée bus stop on the Avenue du Grand-Saint-Bernard, back-track slightly towards the river and turn onto the Route de la Croix. At the busy road, highway 21, go left in order to cross it and continue on what becomes Route de Plan-Cerisier. Take the second right, which is a shortcut footpath that rejoins Route de Plan-Cerisier just before the first houses of the old village. Walk up through the collection of tightly packed houses – the tiny museum is on the right after the road splits (parking lot on the left). Wander through the houses and walk back to the Plan-Cerisier road, then explore a second set of houses before taking the road, which ends shortly after the restaurant of the same name.

The street turns into a footpath through the vines, called Les Guières after the name of this section of vineyard. These are some of the most remarkable drystone walls in Valais, beautiful as the seasons change and visible from much of the Rhone valley. Parts of the trail here are one-person wide, with walls and vineyards above and below. Continue for some distance

with the main road to the Forclaz Pass continually drawing closer. When the trail comes to a small road from the left and above, follow it until shortly before the Forclaz road (above and on the left): the farm road goes up to join it but the footpath that the trail follows goes to the right now. Note that this part of the trail will be retraced. Cross a lower section of the generally busy Forclaz road.

The trail does a small loop at the ruins. Follow the same path back but take a short loop to the left when it appears, away from the vineyards above. Rejoin the trail and continue straight, crossing the Forclaz road in the same place as before. At the junction of the footpath and the small farm road, take the right-hand option to begin climbing up to an area aptly called Le Sommet des Vignes, the top of the vineyards, before forest and cliff take over. Soon after the path splits it crosses the looping Forclaz road again and heads towards a collection of houses, crossing a small farm road, Route du Sommet des Vignes, then skirting the lower end of the buildings. Ignore all small roads, continuing on what is now Chemin des Rives, until the trail comes to a small winding road that leads up to a group of villages above the trail. Take the road briefly, but when a footpath to the left appears, follow it to begin the downhill trek towards the vineyards. This part of the trail cuts through woods with some fine, tall old trees. Simply follow the path – there are no other options – until vineyards and a farm appear on the left. Soon after, the footpath ends; take the path to the left for a few metres until it joins the Plan-Cérisier road. Follow this down through the vines, coming out at the lower hamlets of Plan-Cérisier, not far from the restaurant and hamlets visited at the start of the hike. At the T-junction turn left and very quickly turn right onto a street, Rue du Perrey. Follow it down through the village and out the lower end towards Martigny Croix, staying on this small road until it splits. Take the right-hand option, Rue des Ecottins. Follow signs for Les Rappes until the five-way intersection: take the second right to climb up Rue du Village – alternatively, take the even steeper Route des Rappes and consider

that this was once the stagecoach road! Both streets end at Route de la Combe, with the Besse winery easy to spot between them.

### Return
Bus or walk down to Martigny, 15 minutes. When walking up to the winery, note the bus stop on Route de la Combe, just metres from the winery.

### Notes
Mazot-Musée de Plan-Cérisier is known as the smallest vine museum in Switzerland. Despite its tiny size it is an excellent way to learn about this very unusual small village, where inhabitants of the Val de Trient villages high above came down with mules in the past to work their vines and harvest the grapes before trekking back up later with their wine. Several of the old houses in larchwood with slate roofs are still here. The museum is open two evenings a week in summer, or by appointment.

This area is part of the ancient trails system over the St. Bernard Pass, a region sometimes known as the Golden Triangle, where France, Italy and Switzerland come together.

Dog friendly hike, but the path is one-person wide in many areas.

# GÉRALD BESSE WINERY

Gérald Besse is a self-taught mountain vigneron who began to buy vine parcels in 1979. He and his wife, Patricia, opened the winery in 1984. Since then, the cellar has earned a reputation for fine mineral wines from the granite soils of the Mont Blanc range and for a strong commitment to maintaining this special soil and the daunting drystone walls that support the vineyards. Their children have joined them in the past decade, notably Sara, who has a degree in viticulture/oenology engineering, working full-time as the winery reconverts to organic winemaking. The combination has resulted in the winery being listed as one of the country's best in several reviews; its Ermitage Martigny Vieille Vigne Les Serpentines wine is part of the prestigious Mémoire des Vins Suisses collection.

 **Gamay St. Théodule:** The winery makes three Gamay wines and several other reds; their expertise with this grape in particular is evident. This one is the top of the line for the three, but the others are equally pleasing, if lighter.

## ADDRESS

**Domaine Gérald Besse SA**
Route de la Combe 14
Les Rappes
1921 Martigny-Croix
Tel: 027 722 7881
info@besse.ch
besse.ch

## WINERY FEES

No. Open regular hours.

## WHERE ELSE TO FIND THIS CELLAR'S WINES NEARBY

**Restaurant de Plan-Cerisier**, Les Guières 15, 1921 Martigny-Croix, 027 722 25 29
info@plan-cerisier.ch

# FULLY

## GEOGRAPHY OF THE ALPS GALORE!

LOWER VALAIS

| ▷··· STARTING POINT | ···✗ DESTINATION |
|---|---|
| **BRANSON, PONT DU RHÔNE POSTAL BUS STOP** | **CAVE LA RODELINE, FULLY** |

| 📅 SEASON | 🎴 HIKE TYPE |
|---|---|
| **YEAR-ROUND** <br> UNLESS THERE IS SNOW | **MODERATE /DIFFICULT**   |

| ⛰ MAP REFERENCE | ⏱ DURATION |
|---|---|
| **SHEET 272T** | **3H 45M** |

| | ↦ LENGTH |
|---|---|
| | **11.7 KM** |

| 🔍 INTERESTING SIGHTS | 〰 CLIMB / DESCENT |
|---|---|
| RHONE CANAL. <br> COMBE D'ENFER. <br> WALNUT FOREST. | **625 M / 626 M** |

## LA MURGÈRE
## PETITE ARVINE
### DOMAINE LA RODELINE

 WHITE

 RHUBARB,
FLOWERING WISTERIA,
SOME CITRUS

 FRESH, MINERAL,
LIVELY WITH THE PERFECT
SALINE FINISH THAT IS
TYPICAL FOR THIS GRAPE

 DRY,
STILL

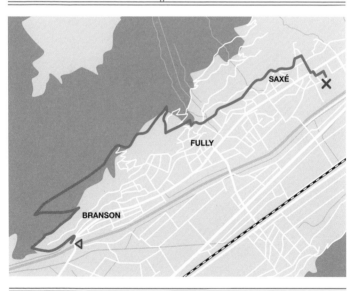

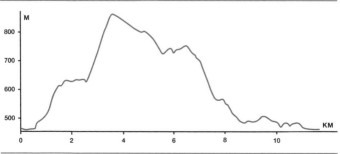

# DESCRIPTION OF THE ROUTE

From the bus stop cross the Fully canal by following the footpath to take the footbridge. Turn left onto Chemin de Clos des Follatères. Follow it uphill; soon after a footpath to the left, the trail makes a sharp right and continues for some time, going above the vineyards. At a Y-junction, stay left. At the next Y-junction stay right (continue straight). At the next rough T-junction, in an area of open brush, take a sharp left. The first houses of Branson, on the outskirts of Fully, are not far below.

Follow the trail uphill, a climb of some 200 metres with a zigzag which comes immediately after a trail that heads right. The trail then meets up with the small road Route de Jeur Brûlée; stay on this for some distance. When the road bends sharply to the right to go downhill, continue straight on the farm road: you have reached the impressive and accurately named Combe d'Enfer, a very special place for growing

grapes because the deep curve in the landscape provides such different sun expositions. The trail goes along the top of most of the vineyard and above a small collection of old houses, Tassonnières. When the path reaches Chemin de Plamont, follow it to the left. Continue through the vines for some distance until a marked trail, Chemin des Avasiers, and taking a very sharp right, follow it downhill: this leads to a well-known rendezvous spot with a large cross and a few parking spaces.

At the cross take the footpath that heads downhill. It eventually joins Sentier Tassonnières Rappe (take this to the left), which becomes a small road. When it ends, cross over Chemin des Avasiers and when the trail splits right afterwards, take the left-hand option. Where the trail intersects with another turn right, and cross over another trail. Turn left at Chemin des Bogues, take the first footpath to the right and stay to the right then turn left at the small T-junction just before Route d'Euloz. Cross the parking lot and at the bottom end follow the footpath – do not go right – and cross Chemin de l'Usine, pick up Chemin de la Treille and when it turns right continue straight along the footpath to Châtaignier. In the 1798 census this was the most populated village in the area, 129 souls.

At this point the trail has moved out of the higher vineyards and continues to head east (in the direction of Sion) in a more or less straight line along footpaths and small farm roads to La Fin de Saxé (12 homes were wiped out by a landslide and flood in 1939) and Mazembroz. Shortly before the latter, turn onto Chemin du Poubloz and soon after take the footpath to the right that leads to the main street, Chemin de la Comballe, which becomes Rue Saint-Gothard. Cross the canal and the Route de Martigny on the other side. Take the first left, which bends right, Chemin des Clares. Take the first left then the third right and the winery is on the left.

**Return**

The main street of Fully, with bus service, is a 5-minute walk.

**Notes**

A nice detour at the start of the hike: instead of starting to climb on the footpath, follow the small road next to the canal, away from Fully, to see the elbow in the Rhone. There is a small covered footbridge here and immediately after, a white sand waterfront alongside the canal. The vines to the right are organic, in nearly virgin condition.

Combe d'Enfer is one of the most daunting vineyard areas in Switzerland, extremely hot in summer, very steep even by alpine standards, with drystone walls that are under constant pressure from the mountain. It's a wonder that anyone wants to grow grapes here, and indeed it was mostly abandoned until two decades ago, when a handful of top vignerons from Fully went to work restoring it, knowing the quality of the grapes from here would be quite special.

# DOMAINE LA RODELINE

Claudine and Yvon Roduit make some of the finest terroir wines in Fully, a town that has an abundance of good wineries. Their focus for 40 years has been on understanding the relationship between the land and the vines. She is the grower, overseeing the vineyards, and he is the oenologist, overseeing the winemaking, but beyond that they have a great depth of knowledge about the surrounding fauna and flora, the rocks and soils of what many consider the most extraordinary mountainside in a region of great alpine beauty. It's not surprising that their wine tourism offer includes guided hikes and nature walks to explain the vineyards here in a larger context.

 **La Murgère Petite Arvine:** This is a classic Petite Arvine with its sharp yet very pleasing notes of rhubarb and a finish that makes it clear what a salty or saline wine is. This is one of the best wineries in Valais for learning about Petite Arvine, simply by comparing their three distinctively different ones, each reflecting a terroir, none quite like the others. Ask why, and the answer reflects what the trail shows.

## ADDRESS

**Domaine La Rodeline**
Chemin des Sablons 11
1926 Fully
**Cave Rodeline**
Rue de la Fontaine 114
1926 Fully
Tel: 079 214 0427
info@rodeline.ch
rodeline.ch

## WINERY FEES

Various options. By appointment.

## WHERE ELSE TO FIND THIS CELLAR'S WINES NEARBY

**Café des Amis**, Rte de Saillon 142, 1926 Fully,
027 746 18 95
**Fol'terres**, Chem. du Rhône 135, 1926 Fully,
027 746 13 13

# SAINT-PIERRE-DE-CLAGES

## TRACKING ROBIN HOOD AKA FARINET

LOWER VALAIS

| ▷··· STARTING POINT | ···✕ DESTINATION |
|---|---|
| **SAILLON BUS STOP: LES MOILLES** | **SIMON MAYE ET FILS, SAINT-PIERRE-DE-CLAGES** |

| 🗓 SEASON | 🧩 HIKE TYPE |
|---|---|
| **YEAR-ROUND** SNOW PERMITTING | **MODERATE**  |

| 🗺 MAP REFERENCE | 🕐 DURATION |
|---|---|
| **SHEET 272T** | **3H 45M** |

| | ⊢ LENGTH |
|---|---|
| | **13.1 KM** |

| 🔍 INTERESTING SIGHTS | 〰 CLIMB / DESCENT |
|---|---|
| CASTLE AND OLD TOWN IN SAILLON. FARINET'S VINEYARD: SMALLEST OFFICIAL ONE IN THE WORLD. FARINET'S FOOTBRIDGE. LA LOSENTSE RIVER. | **585 M / 501 M** |

## SYRAH VIEILLES VIGNES
### SIMON MAYE ET FILS

 RED

 BLACK FRUITS AND SPICES

 COMPLEX, GOOD DEPTH, VERY ELEGANT

 DRY, STILL, MATURED IN OAK FOR A YEAR, THEN SOME MONTHS IN CONCRETE

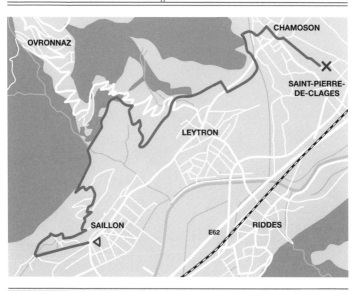

OVRONNAZ

CHAMOSON

SAINT-PIERRE-DE-CLAGES

LEYTRON

SAILLON

RIDDES

E62

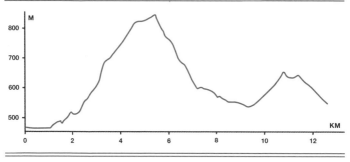

# DESCRIPTION OF THE ROUTE

From the bus stop (Les Moilles), take Vers les Scex, but quickly turn left onto Chemin des Amandiers, away from the village in the direction of Martigny. Continue alongside the canal on Route de Gru until you come to a small bridge; cross over, pass an informal parking area and turn right, starting to climb on the Route de Sinlio, towards the castle. Watch carefully for a narrow footpath to the right, called Sentiers des Chèvres. Stay on this path as it becomes Chemin des Barmes, then Sentier des Anémones. It moves behind the castle tower and leads into the top end of the old village of Saillon.

Turn left at the Route des Chavannes, and turn right onto Ruelle des Champs where there are several yellow arrows pointing to different hiking trails. Continue straight on the steep little footpath just after a house on the left; the alternative is to take the road to the left: they join up soon after the split. Continue on the Route des Combes, which winds

back and forth with a short detour (follow the signs) to the world's smallest cadastral vineyard, Vignoble de Farinet, owned by the Dalai Lama.

Continue up through vineyards until the Passerelle à Farinet – one hour from Saillon bourg to this point. The footbridge, built in 2001, crosses the very narrow Salentse Gorge at 780 m a.s.l. Before the Passerelle and at the end of the farm road (point 715 on Swisstopo maps), the vines end and there is an entrance to light woods via a gate that must be kept closed. Cross the light wooden bridge, which is 136 meters above the ravine.

The walk downhill towards Leytron is straightforward, with the town clearly visible below, on the plain: simply follow the yellow footpath signs, passing through the small villages of Les Places, Montagnon and Produit. Note that the trail does not go into the town of Leytron, but passes above it between Champlan and Cavoucin. On the Route des Prix, turn left onto Route de la Collonge, at 600 m a.s.l. and continue straight. At the Route d'Ovronnaz, the main road, join the road for a few meters then head off to the left on the marked trail that becomes the Impasse Sous les Chênes. Follow the trail as it takes a sharp right and crosses over the Route de Chamoson. The trail joins the small road, Route des Champs Longs, through vineyards until it joins a similar road, Route de Prile: take this road to the left. The trail bends left shortly before La Losentse river and continues upstream. This is a lovely part of the walk with forest just to the left, vineyards below to the right, and the river building up strength and speed further down. Follow the marked trail for La Palud/Chamoson, cross the river and turn right onto Rue de la Losentze, take the first left onto Tiers de Mart, left at the Y-junction onto Chemin Neuf, right at Rue Saint-André, right at Rue Plane-Ville. Just after Rue Centrale on the right follow the road as it bends left (Rue des Plantys) and keep left onto Rue Pré de Monthey, then right at Route de Trémazières which goes through vineyards until reaching the winery, on the right, just before the village center.

## Return
The Chamoson train station is a 15-minute walk.

## Notes
Saillon and the name Joseph-Samuel Farinet are intricately linked. He was a man long sought by the police as a counterfeiter in the 19th century, but who was also a charmer and Swiss Robin Hood who took refuge in Saillon. The legend long ago eclipsed the man, whose body was found at the bottom of the Salentse Gorge in 1880, rumoured to have been laid low by a police bullet. Today a famously tiny vineyard is named after him, as well as a dizzying footbridge over the ravine where he took his last breath. Before the footbridge, locals used a precarious cable system to haul across grapes, tools and more – and they used a daunting *bisse* irrigation canal, built against the rock wall, to bring drinking water down from the peaks to Saillon. A via ferrata below the bridge, a museum, hiking trails, a series of stained glass trail markers, and several artworks all bear his name.

The 21 stained glass trail markers up to the Farinet vines (there are just three) are one of the joys of this walk, recounting the life of mortals and the values treasured by humanity. They are the work of artists Robert Héritier, Théo Imboden, Pascal Thurre.

# SIMON MAYE ET FILS

The winery is known for pushing Valais wines firmly in the direction of quality in the mid-20th century, at a time when quantity was the buzz word and the quality of wines in the region was suffering. Simon Maye studied law and was planning to go abroad, but his father insisted he stay home – in 1948, after he harvested his first grapes and made his first wine, he agreed. Much of the work he did in the following decades went against the received winemaking wisdom of the time, but his products were a success. He founded the Confrérie St. Théodule, whose members are Valais cellars that agree to its quality charter. His two sons proceeded to build the business and anchor the quality reputation, and Raphael, a grandson who trained in wineries in several countries, has recently taken over. The wines are often sold out, such is the demand.

**Syrah Vieille Vignes:** This is a wine that is often hard to find because of limited production and its reputation as one of the best Swiss northern Rhone wines.

## ADDRESS

**Simon Maye et Fils**
Rue de Collombey 3
1955 St-Pierre-de-Clages
Tel: 027 306 4181
info@simonmaye.ch
simonmaye.ch

## WINERY FEES

No. Regular opening hours, but call ahead.

## WHERE ELSE TO FIND THIS CELLAR'S WINES NEARBY

**Café-Restaurant la Pinte**, Rue de l'Eglise 20, 1955 Chamoson, 027 306 25 04
**Le bistrot Saint-André**, Rue Saint-André 11, 1955 Chamoson, 027 306 20 51
bistrot@saint-andre.ch

# SAINT-PIERRE-DE-CLAGES

## RAW BEAUTY FROM RHONE TO RUGGED PEAKS, STREAMS

LOWER VALAIS

| ▷⋯ STARTING POINT | ⋯✕ DESTINATION |
|---|---|
| **CHAMOSON TRAIN STATION/ BUS STOPS** | **DANIEL MAGLIOCCO & FILS SAINT-PIERRE-DE-CLAGES** |

| 🗓 SEASON | 🎟 HIKE TYPE |
|---|---|
| **YEAR-ROUND** UNLESS SNOW | **MODERATE** 🚶 |

| 🗺 MAP REFERENCE | ⏱ DURATION |
|---|---|
| **SHEET 272T** | **3H 15M** |
| | ↦ LENGTH |
| | **11 KM** |

| 🔍 INTERESTING SIGHTS | |
|---|---|
| LES SIX DE GRU CLIFFS. GUERITES (GROWERS' HUTS). CAROLINGIAN ART. ROMANESQUE CHURCH IN SAINT-PIERRE-DE-CLAGES. FAMOUS SECONDHAND BOOKSHOPS. | 〰 CLIMB / DESCENT |
| | **442 M / 413 M** |

## FENDANT
### CAVE DANIEL MAGLIOCCO & FILS

 WHITE

 CITRUS FRUITS, FLINT

 MINERAL, DRY, FRUIT NOTES, SLIGHTLY SOUR REFRESHING FINISH

 DRY, STILL

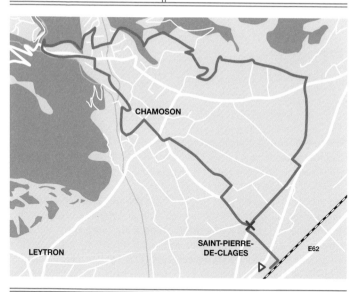

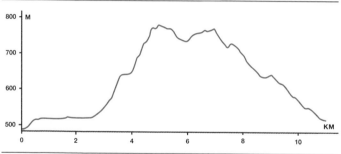

# DESCRIPTION OF THE ROUTE

From the train station, also a main bus stop, head up the hill in a straight line to the village of Saint-Pierre-de-Clages. At the Rue de l'Eglise turn right and note the 11th century Romanesque church – when entering the building step down to the level that was once the entrance but subsidence over the centuries has lowered this by about one metre.

Continue along the Rue de l'Eglise to a Tamoil petrol station on the left and turn left immediately after. Take time here to study the panel about alpine vegetation at different altitudes, an excellent general bit of information. The trail heads through the vines towards the Six de Gru cliff. Turn left at the base and follow the marked footpath parallel to the bottom of the cliff, climbing gently at first then more steeply. Continue on the path as it bends left, above the vineyards and just below a road. The trail weaves around the edge of the vineyards, briefly crossing a road. Simply follow the arrows.

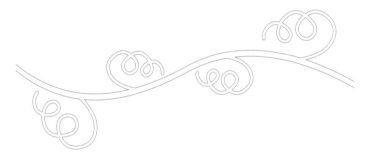

This part of the trail offers a view of the spectacular spread of vineyards in Chamoson, but it hasn't always been so. In the 1960s market gardening and mixed farming gave way to vineyards as the wine market boomed.

The trail goes through the top end of Chamoson, entering a housing area on Rue du Nasot (follow the footpath arrows) at a bridge over a stream. The trail stays on this street, crosses the Tséné River and turns right at the corner of Rue Chez Moren (alternatively, just after the bridge follow the hiking path arrows – they turn right up a footpath, only to arrive at the same point in a couple hundred metres). Follow the signposts for the Bisse du Poteu, taking a footpath to the left. The bisse walk goes along the edge of woods, bends right and takes a hairpin bend to the left before reaching the road Pont Crittin. Stay on the footpath, which runs between the road and La Losentse river, heading back towards Chamoson.

At a clearing with a couple of buildings, a small road to the left, Sentier des Amoureux, veers off from the trail: take this onto Pont Crittin. Take the first right (street) to the T-junction with Chemin du Marqueu and Chemin Proz chez Boz. Turn left. Continue on this street, which bends right, until Route du Châtelard, next to a stream. Stay on this street,

again named Proz chez Boz, to the T-junction; turn right. Take the first right (Rue chez Pottier) then the first left onto Rue de la Losentze.

Take the first left, Tiers de Mart, quickly turn left at Chemin Neuf and right onto Rue Centrale. The trail at this point is a walk through the center of Chamoson. Continue straight at the main intersection and follow the road to the left – called Rue Pré de Monthey now – and take the first right onto Route de Trémazières. The trail is now back among the vineyards, heading gently downhill to Saint-Pierre-de-Clages. At Route des Dahrres, where the houses begin, turn right and take the next left at Rue de Collombey. Follow it into the centre's main intersection and turn right then into the second left; the winery is downhill on the left.

**Return**
Two-minute walk to the bus stop just below Saint-Pierre-de-Clages town square with connections to the train station.

**Notes**
This is a straightforward hike except for the part of the trail where you pick up the Bisse du Poteu at the top of Chamoson. It's easy to miss the signposts, so watch carefully for signs and arrows. This can be a wild area after torrential rains – a massive mudslide hit the top of town in recent years. Until the 1960s most of the area that is now vineyard was used for other forms of agriculture, mainly crops.

A guided visit to the old Romanesque church in Saint-Pierre-de-Clages takes just under an hour and is worthwhile.

# CAVE DANIEL MAGLIOCCO & FILS

The family arrived in this area in 1952. The grandfather was a butcher. Magliocco *père*, Daniel, was 20 when the family bought vines and orchards and market garden land; he built up the winery in the heart of this large wine village, which runs together with Chamoson. Son Mikael, who is an ardent fan of letting the grapes speak for themselves, joined the business in 2006 and oversaw the end of synthetic products in the vineyard in 2015 and the reconversion to organic in 2018. He has strong opinions on minimal intervention and paying very close attention to what each harvest's grapes tell him. He's independent-minded, not interested in fads or wine recipes, is gaining a reputation for quality, and he likes to share his thoughts on what works and what doesn't.

The line-up of wines is interesting and many are surprising – the Fendant has more character than most, mineral and racy. The Gamay has a depth that's unusual. It's not possible to simply taste wine here: you have to be keen to jump into the conversation, and you'll walk away knowing more than when you entered.

 **Fendant:** While the red wines here are perhaps the specialty, this is, in a good year, one of the most interesting Fendants in the region, with real character.

## ADDRESS

**Magliocco & Fils**
Av. de la Gare 10
1955 Saint-Pierre-de-Clages
Tel: 079 445 8888
daniel@maglioccovins.ch
mikael@maglioccovins.ch
maglioccovins.ch

## WINERY FEES

No

## WHERE ELSE TO FIND THIS CELLAR'S WINES NEARBY

**Le 1955**, Rue de l'Eglise 19, 1955 Saint-Pierre-de Clages,
027 565 55 54
info@le1955.ch
**OH!Berge Planeville**, Rue de Plane Ville 24, 1955 Chamoson,
027 306 60 30
ohberge@planeville.ch
**Le bistrot Saint-André**, Rue Saint-André 11, 1955 Chamoson,
027 306 20 51
bistrot@saint-andre.ch
**La Potagère**, Rue de l'Eglise 3, 1955 Saint-Pierre-de-Clages,
027 306 43 44
info@potagere.ch

# VÉTROZ

## THE WILD SIDE, A DEEP FOLD IN THE ALPS

LOWER VALAIS

---

▷⋯ **STARTING POINT**

**CHANDOLIN, SAVIÈSE CENTRAL PLAZA BUS STOP**

⋯✕ **DESTINATION**

**CAVE DE LA MADELEINE, VÉTROZ**

 **SEASON**

**MAY-NOVEMBER** FOR THE ENTIRE ROUTE. FROM DAILLON TO VÉTROZ, ABOUT 4 KM SHORTER, IS POSSIBLE YEAR-ROUND DEPENDING ON SNOW CONDITIONS.

**HIKE TYPE**

**DIFFICULT**

**MAP REFERENCE**

# SHEET 273T

🕐 **DURATION**

## 3H 45M

↦ **LENGTH**

## 13.1 KM

🔍 **INTERESTING SIGHTS**

CHANDOLIN: DUMOULIN HOUSE.
NOTRE DAME DES CORBELINS.
PONT DU DIABLE.
VÉTROZ, PLACE DU FOUR.

〰 **CLIMB / DESCENT**

## 723 M / 388 M

**AMIGNE GRAND CRU (2 BEES)**
CAVE DE LA MADELEINE

WHITE

FLORAL AND FOREST HONEYS, ORANGES, KUMQUATS

RICH, SMOOTH INITIALLY, CITRUS FRUITS AND FRUIT JAMS, NOTICEABLE ACIDITY TOWARDS THE END THAT GIVES IT LENGTH — BALANCED, HARMONIOUS

SLIGHTLY SWEET

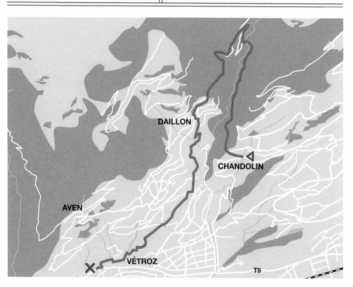

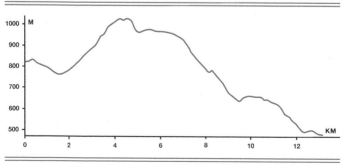

# DESCRIPTION OF THE ROUTE

From the bus stop at the center of Chandolin, Savièse, head west along the main street, the Route du Sanetsch, past village landmarks with explanatory panels including the Dumoulin family house and the home of famous son Basile Luyet. At an intersection with a bus stop, one road goes uphill towards the Tsanfleuron Glacier while the main road heads steeply downhill, and here the view opens out spectacularly onto the Morge ravine and Conthey's seemingly vertical vineyards on the other side, as well as peaks in three cantons. The road moves past the Notre Dame de Corbelin chapel, then the village dump and recycling center, both on the left. At this point the road dips steeply and in winter it remains in the shade most of the day. Continue for some distance until reaching the Pont du Diable, built in 1655.

The trail here loops back to go along the right bank of the river. Follow signs for Daillon and Sensine, climbing back up another steep section of the Route du Sanetsch. At Pomeiron the road begins to drop down gently again. Continue on the Sanetsch road, which has several hairpin bends in Daillon. Immediately after a bend to the left (Route des Nez goes off to the right), take a small road down towards an area called La Vella, following Rue du Morey until it splits and the left fork is called Rue de la Vella. Continue on this small vineyard road, down through the vines – Chandolin and the chapel are across the ravine – always staying on the path (twice it veers left at small intersections) until the top end of Sensine. Cross over Route de la Blanchette, a larger road, and continue on what is now Rue de Somvellaz.

Midway through the village take a right onto Rue de Vaux. When it splits, follow the left-hand path and for some time continue on this vineyard road, through the vines. Just above the hamlet of St. Séverin, the trail crosses and very briefly joins Chemin de Plan d'Avé. Pick up the vineyard path heading downhill and to the left as the road splits.

The trail now goes through the vineyards, but watch for a yellow trail sign that leads off the road, the first turn to the left, and down a path that quickly becomes dirt. It bends right, goes to a vigneron's hut, where the trail makes a sharp right then left down next to a small canal. In Vétroz head west on Rue des Vignerons to the main place near the church, then above the church and continue onto Route de l'Abbaye, which bends left and soon joins the Route Cantonale. Turn right; the winery is a few meters further on the right.

**Return**
Vétroz has a bus stop a five-minute walk from the winery, on the main road to the village center.

**Notes**
Chandolin – not to be confused with another high Alpine village and resort of the same name, in the Val d'Anniviers – has the air of belonging to a deep valley with no outlet, but it is actually on the road to the Col de Sanetsch. Cantons Vaud (Diablerets), Valais and Bern meet in this area, from which water flows down to Valais via the Morge river and on the other side to Bern to join the Rhine via the Aare river.

Notre-Dame des Corbelins was the final one of three chapels on a pilgrimage made by women whose babies were born dead or died soon after; in the Catholic Church at the time it was believed these children went to Limbo. The chapel was reputed to be a place where the Virgin Mary would give these children life again, just long enough to allow them to be baptized and thus sent to Paradise for eternity. It was built onto a large rock in 1655 and also served as a place where those traveling into the wilder areas ahead asked for protection; it was renovated in 1989.

Another landmark in the village is the home of Basile Luyet, a native son whose lifelong research into life and death at low temperatures led to the new field in science known as cryobiology.

In 1942 a drama occurred in Chandolin. The parents of seven children, the Dumoulins, left home, putting the eldest in charge, to check on their cows in high pastures above the village. They took a shortcut across the glacier and disappeared. Their bodies were covered by snow and ice until 2017 when the retreating glacier freed them and the bodies were discovered. Their house is one of the first landmarks with a plaque on the trail.

Pont du Diable: legend has it that putting a bridge over the Morge river was so impossible a task that the devil had to be called in. He agreed to do the job but in return villagers had to promise that he could have the ninth soul that crossed the bridge. After number eight, along came a man and his dog – the animal was thrown onto the bridge, tricking the furious devil.

This hike can be extended to include the Torrent Neuf, also called the Bisse de Savièse, long considered one of the most spectacular of the Valais *bisses*. Allow one hour to reach the *bisse* and another 2.5–3 hours to walk along it – the *bisse* trail is easy but decidedly vertiginous in places.

# CAVE DE LA MADELEINE

André Fontannaz created the winery in 1991 but from the start it has been a family business. His sister (local stained glass artist Isabelle Fontannaz) created the artwork that is part of the logo and labels, and most recently daughters Camille and Chloé have joined the cellar. In just 30 years this has become one of the most respected wineries in Switzerland, contributing significantly to the international renown of Amigne. The Fontannaz family has earned a reputation for excellent terroir and traditional wines from several grapes. The number of often award-winning oaked wines and those made at least in part in amphores has increased in the past decade. The Amigne Vétroz Grand Cru is from grapes grown on the lower slopes above the village in the oldest vine parcel in Vétroz.

 **Amigne Grand Cru (2 bees):** Amigne is a very old and special grape that lends itself equally well to dry wines and naturally sweeter ones. The only place in the world where it is grown is Valais, and Vétroz accounts for 70% of the canton's Amigne. This is also the only grape variety in Switzerland where the sugar level must be listed on the label. Vétroz wineries have been using an easy three-bee logo system since 2006: a drawing of one bee is a dry wine (0–8 g of residual sugar per litre), two bees indicate medium-dry to medium-sweet (9–25 g RS/l) and three is sweet, generally a late harvest wine from grapes picked in December or January, whose sugar concentration builds naturally (25+ g RS/l); it generally ages beautifully for several years. The Fontannaz family here makes several versions of Amigne, making this an excellent place to sample, compare and learn.

## ADDRESS

**La Madeleine - André Fontannaz et Filles**
Route Cantonale 118,
1963 Vétroz
Tel: 027 346 46 54
info@fontannaz.ch
fontannaz.ch

## WINERY FEES

CHF15, free if you buy wine. Regular opening hours.

## WHERE ELSE TO FIND THIS CELLAR'S WINES NEARBY

**Relais du Valais**, Rte de l'Abbaye 35, 1963 Vétroz,
027 346 03 03
**Café La Madeleine**, Av. des Vergers 20, 1963 Vétroz,
027 346 10 11

# SION

## PURE GOLD, GOING BACK MILLENNIA

CENTRAL VALAIS

▷⋯ **STARTING POINT**

DRÔNE, SAVIÈSE
VILLAGE CENTER BUS STOP

⋯✕ **DESTINATION**

DOMAINE DU MONT D'OR,
SION

📅 **SEASON**

**YEAR-ROUND** (ICE POSSIBLE
ON SOME SECTIONS IN WINTER)

🗺 **MAP REFERENCE**

# SHEET 273T

🔎 **INTERESTING SIGHTS**

BISSE DE LENTINE VINEYARD WATERING SYSTEM.
MONT D'ORGE LAKE AND NATURE RESERVE.
MONT D'OR CASTLE RUINS.

🏃 **HIKE TYPE**

# MODERATE

🕐 **DURATION**

# 2H 30M

↦ **LENGTH**

〰 **CLIMB / DESCENT**

# 90 M / 444 M

## ST. MARTIN GRAIN NOBLE
MONT D'OR

WHITE

NOTHING SHY HERE:
CORINTH RAISINS,
BITTER ALMONDS

POWERFUL, NOTES OF GRAPE
CONFITURE, LUSCIOUSLY
SWEET YET FRESH,
WITH GOOD ACIDITY AND
A VERY LONG FINISH

SWEET,
STILL

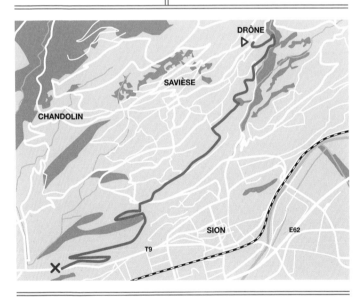

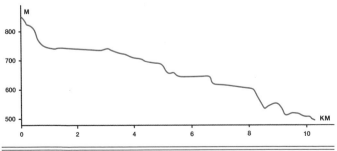

# DESCRIPTION OF THE ROUTE

Drône, part of Savièse, has one main street. Walk a few metres south-west to Ruelle du Boulanger, turn left after the T-junction and continue downhill on the same path where Ruelle du Boulanger continues to the left, go down through the vines, look for signposts for Pont de la Sionne, Grimisuat, Bisse de Lentine. This is a popular family walk and mostly well-marked. The trail continues to head down until it joins the irrigation canal, or *bisse*; turn right to walk along the bisse.

The trail is easy to follow from here – simply follow the bisse itself and bisse signs. When the trail reaches a housing area, the water goes underground, surfacing again at Mont d'Orge Lake.

At this point follow signs for the 15-minute walk around the lake, starting at the top end. The trail comes out next to two parking lots and several hiking path signposts, which can be confusing, given the

number of similar-sounding paths. Look for arrows to the Montorge bisse trail, the only one to lead steeply downhill. This is a patch that can be icy and messy in winter, but with stairs and a ramp option, it is manageable and continues only for a couple hundred meters like this. The trail, initially concrete, bends around to the right, in front of stone walls; note a small stone house – the vine in front of it is more than 200 years old. Continue on the path until it reaches the start of the Bisse de Montorge.

The trail is very easy to follow from here, in part because the vineyards and the winery below are visible most of the time. It heads west in a fairly straight line for some distance but then turns abruptly back east in a sharp bend. A similar loop reverses the trail again, coming downhill straight to the winery. The winery has created an educational short vineyard trail of its own; this trail runs along only part of it, but for those wanting to walk a bit more after a tasting session, doing the winery's loop, especially using their very good app, is a nice addition.

**Return**
Buses stop in front of the winery on the outskirts of Sion.

**Notes**

This is one of the most accessible walks alongside a fully functioning and relatively young bisse in Valais, through mostly open countryside for the first section, then through a nature reserve where the Lentine bisse feeds into Montorge Lake, down along a lower and in summer much hotter bisse walk from the lake to nearly level with the Rhone. Each bisse section is still used to water vineyards in this very dry and very sunny part of Switzerland. The Lentine trail in summer offers welcome shade and cool patches next to the water until it leaves the oak forest, when the sun can bear down on hikers. The Mont d'Or trail is very narrow in parts, runs next to high vineyard walls, and the terracing is sometimes steep: this part of the trail is not recommended with very young children.

The Lentine bisse was built between 1860 and 1895, and the Mont d'Or bisse was built privately in 1859–1860 to carry water to the domain's vineyards. The area is steeped in Swiss history. It was, for centuries, at the center of a religious–military–political tug of war between Savoie rulers and the bishops of Sion, among others. The German–French language line sat here only two centuries ago, before retreating up the valley to the far side of Sierre, and patois was still very much the language used high up in the side valleys across from Sion.

The Mont d'Orge nature reserve has hosted numerous research projects that continue to uncover a remarkable history. Rare water plants here have been transplanted to a nursery project in hopes of encouraging the species to survive. The history of wine has benefited from research here that lifted sediment from the lake; analysis of pollen showed that wild grapevines were here in 10,000 BC, but cultivated grapes appeared in the 8th century B.C. – raising questions about the supposed role of Rome in spreading winemaking north through Europe. The trail does not include the hike up to the chateau, although it is possible to add this loop.

# MONT D'OR

The winery's vineyards cover 24 hectares that are all together, a rarity in a country where most wineries have a patchwork of small vineyards. The entire domain sits inside the nationally recognized "natural site" of Montorge, which includes Mont d'Orge.

The winery was created in 1848 by a military man from canton Vaud and is now owned by the Vaud-based Schenk group. It remains, nevertheless, an emblem of the best in Valais wines and production is very much artisanal, with hand harvesting and crafted wines that win top international awards. Its 200 terraced vine parcels, supported by 15 km of dry stone walls (if you lined them up), are dotted by 12 small gold workers' huts, called *guérites*, a reminder that this heritage is a combination of nature's diversity and the hard labour of humans over centuries. St. Martin is a wine made from grapes grown on La Crête des Maladaires, at the south end of the vineyards. Johannisberg is the king grape here, planted on half of the land.

Most of the wines are vinified and then aged in large oval oak vats called *foudres* (*vases* in canton Vaud) in a 19th century cellar built into the rock.

 **St. Martin Grain Noble:** Grain Noble wines are among the world's most treasured dessert wines: rare and naturally sweet from raisined late harvest grapes that have developed Noble Rot from the fungus *Botrytis cinerea*. Valais is one of the world's best locations for this kind of wine, produced only in years when weather permits and in small quantities. Mont d'Or is one of the main cellars of the Grain Noble Confiden-Ciel group of Valais producers of these wines, which can be made only from five grapes and vines that are at least 15 years old; stiff rules and inspections guarantee quality. The wine must be matured at least one year in oak. Mont d'Or is an excellent place to learn about these and to compare different versions from different grapes. Be sure to try the dry version, *Siccus*, for the best demonstration of what this grape, grown on half of the vineyard here, is capable of offering.

## ADDRESS

**Domaine du Mont d'Or**
Rue de Savoie 64
CH 1951 Sion
Tel: 027 346 2032
info@montdor.ch
montdor.ch

## WINERY FEES

A series of fees (CHF12–28) depending on the number of wines, with the possibility of different cheeses. Includes a tour of the winery. Minimum of five people, reservation required. Minimum six persons: guided hiking tour of the vineyards and winery followed by a tasting session.

## WHERE ELSE TO FIND THIS CELLAR'S WINES NEARBY

**Le Caveau Mont d'Or**, Rue de Savoie 64, 1962 Sion,
027 525 28 28
info@caveaumontdor.ch
**Relais du Simplon**, Route de Savoie 84, 1962 Pont-de-la-Morge (Sion),
027 203 11 03
relaisdusimplon@bluewin.ch

# FLANTHEY

## GLACIERS WATER THE VINES, SAFE SAND IN THE SOIL

CENTRAL VALAIS

| ▷⋯ STARTING POINT | ⋯✕ DESTINATION |
|---|---|
| **GRANGES, AVENUE DE LA GARE BUS STOP** | **CAVE LA ROMAINE, FLANTHEY** |
| 📅 SEASON | 🧗 HIKE TYPE |
| **YEAR-ROUND** | **MODERATE** 🚶 |
| ⛰ MAP REFERENCE | 🕐 DURATION |
| **SHEET 272T** | **3H 15M** |
| | ↦ LENGTH |
| 🔍 INTERESTING SIGHTS | **11.1 KM** |
| WELL-KNOWN CLOS AND VINEYARDS. CLOS DE TSAMPÉHRO. CHÂTEAU DE VAAS CULTURAL AND WINE CENTER. | 〰 CLIMB / DESCENT |
| | **467 M / 360 M** |

**SYRAH**
**LES EMPEREURS**
CAVE LA ROMAINE

RED

INTENSE – WARM SPICES,
BLACK BERRIES,
NOTES OF ROASTING

COMPLEX, WITH SPICES (BLACK
PEPPER, CLOVE, NUTMEG) AND
BLUEBERRIES. EXCELLENT
TANNINS, GOOD STRUCTURE,
VELVETY AND RICH FINISH.

DRY,
STILL

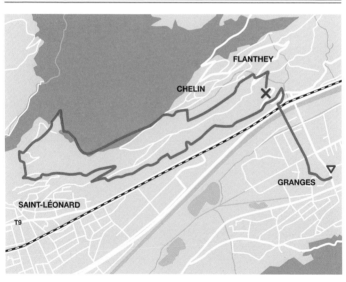

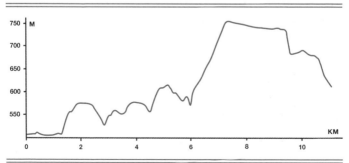

# DESCRIPTION OF THE ROUTE

From the bus stop in Granges, with the castle ruins in front of you, turn left onto Rue de Fauporte and keep left at Rue du Château to skirt the village center. Stay on this street and cross the small Canal Neuf; the street becomes Avenue de la Gare. Continue straight, crossing Rue du Grand Canal and the water until you come to the Rhone at the Route de Poutafontana. Take the footbridge over the Rhone – a short jog to the right and follow signs to cross over the highway, railroad tracks and road that goes up to Ollon. Turn right just over the road and follow the steep and narrow little footpath up to and over Route de Granges. When a larger footpath appears take it to the left and continue straight – the trail joins and then leaves the Route de Granges at what is called the Chemin de Napoléon (in 1810 Valais came under French control with Sion as the seat of the Simplon Département).

The trail continues more or less straight, above the cliffs, over a small gorge bridge with vineyards to the right, including the well-known Mangold vines, where the path changes name, Route d'Orgival. Continue straight – the rock quarry in St. Léonard is below. When the footpath joins a road, Route de Lens, take it to the left and when it intersects the Route des Virets, take that road to the right. Follow this as it makes a hairpin turn to the left and stay on it until it merges with Route du Petit Paradis. Soon after, take the footpath Ruelle des Combettes through the vines towards a small collection of houses, but turn right onto Chemin de Sonville, also a footpath, just before the houses. Take the short footpath to the right soon after, which joins Route du Petit Paradis, then turn left onto the footpath Chemin des Réverettes; when it splits go to the right to rejoin Route du Petit Paradis, turning left to go uphill.

Soon after, take the footpath Chemin du Sillonin to the right and continue to climb; the footpath becomes Impasse du Petit Paradis. The trail takes a sharp right as it reaches the Impasse du Bisse, which is the start of the pleasant Sillonin Bisse walk. Follow this until the trail meets the Route de l'Ormy; take it a few metres and turn off to the right along Chemin des Bouillès. At a Y-junction take the right-hand option along Chemin des Vergers, but at the first footpath to the right take this downhill to join a farm road, Chemin de Lonzemarenda. Continue

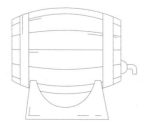

straight, passing the historically significant Clos de Tsampéhro vines (be sure to ask about it at the winery). Carry on until the road, turn right and take it through the village of Vaas-d'en-Bas, with the beautifully restored small Château de Vaas on the right. From here it's a straightforward walk along the road down to the winery, easily visible below. The trail, however, follows a marked footpath just before the first big bend in the road to cut out a large loop. Rejoin the road after the footpath and the winery is on the right.

**Return**
Bus service from the village, a 10-minute walk uphill.

**Notes**
The Sillonin Bisse walk included in this trail is not particularly difficult, whereas the higher part of it, west of this trail, is both spectacular and not for anyone with a fear of heights or falling rocks. Water runs in the bisse from about April to November.

A particularity of the Clos de Tsampéhro area is the discovery of very old vines that were never touched by the grapevine killer phylloxera, which wiped out Europe's vines in the 19th century. Researchers believe it may have been due to deposits of Sahara sand dumped by high-travelling winds behind a ledge here which protected the soil.

# CAVE LA ROMAINE

Joël and Edith Briguet built this modern winery in 1992 and quickly made a name for themselves as extremely hard workers – building the cellar, creating a large lineup of wines with four distinct labels, hosting numerous events and then creating with three others the high-end Clos de Tsampéhro historic wine project on the premises while adding a large barrel room. Behind all this busyness is an excellent winemaker who works with 24 grapes in a stretch from Sion to Sierre, many from some of the most renowned vineyards in the region. It's worth allowing time for a tour of the cellar, particularly the beautiful contemporary barrel room where Clos de Tsampéhro wines age. The wine selected here is Syrah, a fine example of what Swiss north of northern Rhone wines are now achieving. If there is an opportunity, be sure to taste the Cornalin Réserve, a beautiful bemedaled wine that may well be sold out. Visitors are likely to meet the newest member of the team, daughter Adeline, who recently joined the winery after completing a business and economics degree.

 **Syrah Les Empereurs:** The best of the Syrah designed for the Empereurs brand ends up as the award-winning Syrah Réserve. If you are able (they can be out of stock), taste both to compare them.

## ADDRESS

**Cave La Romaine**
Route de Granges 124
3978 Flanthey
Tel: 027 458 4622
info@cavelaromaine.ch
cavelaromaine.com
for Clos de Tsampéhro: clostsampehro.com

## WINERY FEES

No. Regular hours.

## WHERE ELSE TO FIND THIS CELLAR'S WINES NEARBY

**L'Instinct Restaurant**, Route d'Ollon 2, 3977 Granges,
027 458 33 36
info@linstinct.ch
**Château de Vaas – Œnothèque – Maison des cornalins**,
Chemin du Tsaretton 46, 3978 Flanthey,
027 458 11 74
info@chateaudevaas.ch

# SIERRE

## HIGHEST STONE WALLS TO RHONE WALK

CENTRAL VALAIS

| ▷··· STARTING POINT | ···✗ DESTINATION |
|---|---|
| **GRIMISUAT, LES COMBES BUS STOP** | **DOMAINE DES CRÊTES, CHALAIS/NOËS** |
| 🗓 SEASON | 🎲 HIKE TYPE |
| **YEAR-ROUND** | **MODERATE** 🚶 |
| 🗺 MAP REFERENCE | 🕐 DURATION |
| **SHEET 273T** | **5H** |
| | ↦ LENGTH |
| | **19.9 KM** |
| 🔍 INTERESTING SIGHTS | ∿ CLIMB / DESCENT |
| EUROPE'S HIGHEST DRYSTONE WALL. HISTORIC SION OLD TOWN. POUTAFONTANA MIGRATORY BIRD RESERVE. | **81 M / 390 M** |

# FENDANT
## DOMAINE LES CRÊTES

 WHITE

 WHITE FLOWERS,
SOME CITRUS FRUIT

 PLEASANTLY FRESH AND
A GREAT EXAMPLE
OF CHASSELAS FROM
LIMESTONE SOIL

 DRY,
STILL

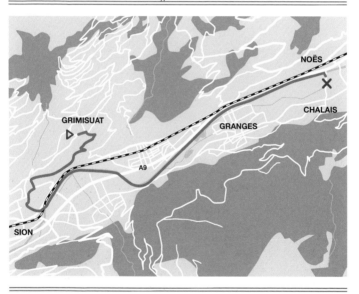

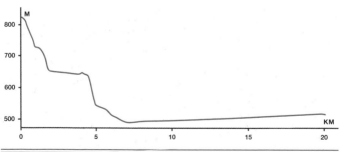

# DESCRIPTION OF THE ROUTE

The 353 and 351 buses from Sion train station show you the spread of vines in all directions in the capital of Switzerland's largest wine-producing canton. Ask the driver to stop at Grimisuat Les Combes in order to enjoy the open part of the *bisse* walk before it hugs the high stone walls.

The bisse (irrigation channel) is not visible from the outset; the path heads downhill to join it, through vines with magnificent views of the Rhone, Sion, vineyards and mountain ranges. The bisse from Signèse to Sion is one of the most popular of these trails, so expect company. Pass below Institute St. Raphael, a school for children in difficulty, from which you suddenly spot the bisse. The walk from the join-up point to the end is easy with beautiful views.

A rusty-looking large block to the right as the path narrows is the Swiss Heritage award-winning Cube, a former *guerite* (one-time growers' hut) where the Celliers de Sion winery organises multi-sensorial tastings. The drystone walls become higher, the path narrower and the drop-off steeper as the vineyards themselves become increasingly spectacular. In the region, the oldest mention of these walls is mid-14th century. Here, the highest drystone walls in Europe tower above you at Cochetta, 12 to 22 meters, built in the 19th century. Educational panels sponsored by wineries are a good distraction. Further along, a restaurant, Brûlefer (also once a guerite) and a groups-only tasting space are wedged in among the vines, the latter reachable through a cave in Champlan village.

The trail opts for a shortcut into Sion before the end of the bisse. The walk is steep but short. Turn off to the left at a metal pole that was once a signpost. It signals the descent to Chemin du Mont. This offers some of the finest views of Sion's famous twin hilltops, the Tourbillon castle ruins and Valère's chateau and basilica, both rich in history. Sion's bishops and feuding religious and lay factions for centuries marked this small city with their money and culture, including some of Switzerland's finest vineyards. Walk down to Rue de Loèche, a busy ring road for the town, and turn left at Rue du Tunnel – go through the tunnel and turn right down one of a number of little narrow streets with museums, boutiques, intriguing architecture: you've reached the Old Town of Sion. Here, the best guide through town to the other side of the Rhone is, remarkably, the bisse – yet it's gone underground! The city's cobblestones include a series of blue ones showing that the water is running hidden underneath. Follow this until running water surfaces next to the street where the Sionne river, into which the bisse flows, is now visible. Stay with it until Rue des Aubépines, a left fork, and walk until the roundabout at Avenue de Tourbillon. Turn left and continue until you reach a small park that leads you to a footbridge across the Rhone.

This is where the Rhone walk begins, nearly 15 km of hiking the dike along one of the Rhone's most enjoyable stretches, albeit urbanised nearby. Head past the Sion golf course to where the Borgne river rushes into the Rhone near Bramois, a town notable for its many organic orchards and vegetables. The river once flowed so wildly that it created this immense Alluvial cone that pushes against the northern flank of the Rhone. Engineers pushed it into a narrow channel and dikes were built in the 19th and 20th centuries, but the system no longer ensures good flood control and the river is being partially rewilded.

Continue along the dike walk to Poutafontana, the largest water nature reserve in Valais and a haven for alpine migratory birds, with a viewing station to observe marsh wildlife. Vineyards reappear: note that along the final stretch there are several abrupt hills, the *crêtes* which give the destination winery its name. The winery is on the right, a few meters before Chalais bridge.

**Return**
Bus stop at the sports center next door takes you to Hôtel de Ville in Sierre, very near the train station.

**Notes**
The Bisse de Clavau, before the descent to Sion, has some narrow stretches with steeply terraced vineyard areas, but is all right for everyone except people with a very strong fear of heights.

Sion is a town of treasures, noted for many secret charms. It is worth taking time out to explore, if not mid-hike, later. The excellent information office is easy to find in the main square, La Planta.

# DOMAINE LES CRÊTES

This is a solid family winery whose products are well known in the area, even if the cellar itself is less familiar to the public. The Vocats have until recently concentrated on supplying restaurants with good quality affordable wines. While many family wineries in Switzerland have 5–12 hectares, the Vocats make wine from 30 hectares, with the grapes grown on five lumpy limestone hills, the *crêtes* formed by glacial movements. Grandfather Joseph founded the cellar in 1950, and his son Yves is still involved, but the next generation, Pierre and Martine, trained as oenologist engineers and have joined the business in the past 10 years, bringing fresh ideas about reaching out more directly to consumers.

 **Fendant:** low acidity, easy to drink.

## ADDRESS

**Domaine les Crêtes**
Route de Pont-Chalais 26
3976 Noës
Tel: 027 458 2649
info@domainedescretes.ch
domainedescretes.ch

## WINERY FEES

No fixed fees. By appointment.

## WHERE ELSE TO FIND THIS CELLAR'S WINES NEARBY

**Hôtel de Ville**, Rue du Bourg 14, 3960 Sierre,
027 452 01 11
ville@sierre.ch
**Le Bourgeois**, Av. du Rothorn 2, 3960 Sierre,
027 455 75 33
info@lebourgeois.ch
**Café Restaurant Le Rothorn**, Av. du Général Guisan 7b, 3960 Sierre,
027 455 11 92
lesimplon64@gmail.com

# SIERRE

## WORK THOSE UPHILL MUSCLES! THEN STROLL SIERRE

CENTRAL VALAIS

| ▷··· STARTING POINT | ···✗ DESTINATION |
|---|---|
| **CHALAIS, TÉLÉPHÉRIQUE BUS STOP** | **CAVE MERCIER, SIERRE** |

| 🗓 SEASON | 🏔 HIKE TYPE |
|---|---|
| **MAY-NOVEMBER.** LA DÉRUPE, THE FIRST PART OF THE TRAIL, IS STEEP AND IS NOT MAINTAINED IN WINTER. | **DIFFICULT** |

**⛰ MAP REFERENCE**

**SHEET 273T**

| 🕐 DURATION |
|---|
| **3H 45M** |

| ↦ LENGTH |
|---|
| **12 KM** |

**🔍 INTERESTING SIGHTS**

BOUILLET CHAPEL.
RHONE RIGHT BANK RIVER WALK.
LAC DE GÉRONDE.
TOUR GOUBING RUINS.

| 〰 CLIMB / DESCENT |
|---|
| **894 M / 60 M** |

**CORNALIN**
CAVE MERCIER

RED

COCOA,
DARK CHOCOLATE,
SPICES, BLACK CHERRIES

VELVETY SMOOTH AND
SUBTLY FRUITY,
DEEPLY RICH AS IT AGES,
LONG FINISH

DRY,
STILL

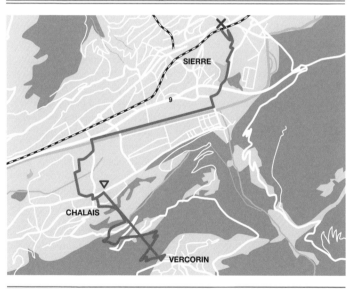

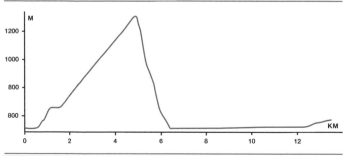

# DESCRIPTION OF THE ROUTE

The trail begins next to the Chalais-Vercorin cable car and winds back and forth under it for much of the climb as far as Briey and the chapel at Bouillet. From the Route de Chippis take the small, parallel Rue du Téléphérique towards the tower ruins; turn left at Rue de la Tour. At the end of the street turn left onto Rue du Fuidjou. Turn right at Chemin des Coudrettes, the start of the trail uphill and into the woods. The trail crosses the Bisse de Réchy, at which point leave the Chemin des Coudrettes trail, which turns left. This steeper trail runs mostly under the cable car here, a climb of about 150 m to the Bisse de Ricard. Turn right and follow the *bisse* (irrigation canal – it goes underground for a while) through vineyards, continue on the marked path as it splits from two others to go left and uphill again, across the main Route de Vercorin. As the vineyards end, the trail bends right and then loops back left, crossing the main road again as it heads towards Briey, which is the cable car mid-station with a collection of houses and farm buildings: the trail crosses the main road yet again just before going under the cable car.

Now begins the steady climb of about 400 m to Vercorin, through forest and occasional open meadows: simply follow the trail – there are no other options. Where the footpath ends and the street begins, turn right along a footpath to the cable car and take it down the mountainside to Chalais, where the trail continues. Walk towards the tower ruins and turn right at the end of the street onto Rue des Chevaliers. At the roundabout take the Route de Granges heading west – signs for Noës and its sports center with football fields and tennis club are on the right as you leave the round-about. Crête du Pont, the larger of the small hills here, is also on the right. After a few metres take a footpath, Route de Raby, to the right to go around the hill. Continue straight, across a small canal, fields on the left. When almost at the level of the football fields, take a small track to the right towards the sports area and continue to just before the football fields; turn left to skirt the fields then take the road to the right at the endof the dirt track, which leads into the parking area: Chemin des Etourneaux.

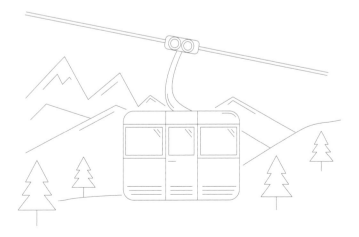

The road leads to an intersection with Rue de Pont Chalais; turn left and cross the bridge over the Rhone into Sierre, then take the small road immediately to the right at the end of the bridge, the Chemin des Peupliers. This is the start of a long, flat, pleasant walk along the Rhone, most of it closed to motorized vehicles, bordered by the Rhone on the right and on the left by a mix of industry (including a large aluminium production complex), farmland, castle ruins and vineyards. Stay on the riverfront path until the busy road next to a bridge; turn left here, at the Technopole business center and walk towards the roundabout. Turn right onto Route des Falaises, take the second left and an immediate right to enter the park for the Grand Lac, also called Lac de Géronde. The trail follows the footpath around the lake, on the right-hand side, to the end of the lake, just before the swimming pool; turn right along Chemin des Sources. At the first street, Chemin de Combette, turn left but quickly take a right onto Chemin du Monastère, continuing until it rejoins Combette. Where the street reaches a group of buildings, the narrow Chemin du Cornalin appears, looping back and up the hillside. Follow this street and signs to the winery, turning right before the Tour de Goubing, onto Chemin de Crêt Goubing and follow it to the end, where the winery overlooks Sierre.

**Return**

To the Sierre train station: 15 minutes by bus via Route du Simplon or 18 minutes on foot.

**Notes**

This is an unusual hike for this book because it starts at the bottom of a mountainside, takes you up to a ski resort but then has you come down via the cable car and continue on from your starting point. The original idea was to take the cable car up and begin the hike in Vercorin, walking down. But the slope is very steep and too many people complain that it's a knee-killer and the walk is better going up. In fact, the Chalais-Vercorin trail, known as La Dérube, is well known to hikers but also runners and mountain bikers in competitions – and it's more often done from bottom to top. The cable car runs frequently, year-round. It is also possible to take a bus from Vercorin to Sierre.

Along the Rhone and inside Sierre, there are many clues to the city's somewhat hazy past. The walls of the Vieux Sierre (Siders) castle date to the 13th century. The small lakes in this area (Petit and Grand Lacs) and several lumpy hills that were created by a pre-history landslide above Salgesch hold archaeological evidence from Roman times.

Note that what looks like an unnecessary loop at the end, to reach the winery, really is necessary. There aren't any good shortcuts: do stick to the trail map!

# CAVE MERCIER

The name Mercier is famous in Sierre, for the family chateau overlooks the town. It was built in 1908 as a summer home for the Mercier family in Lausanne, which made its wealth in the tanning business; the home was donated to the canton in 1991. Denis, one of the descendants, and his wife Anne-Catherine took over management of the chateau vineyards in 1981. They began with two grape varieties and 3 hectares of vines around the chateau, but today their winery has more than 7 hectares and 13 types of grapes are grown on several slopes near the town. Their daughter Madeleine, who at the time of writing is the president of the prestigious Mémoire des Vins Suisses group, joined them in 2012 after gaining experience with renowned international wineries abroad. Given their reputation, the quiet family winery in its discreet hilltop setting may come as a surprise. The approach here is a blend of sustainable practices and innovation that includes an underground vaulted cellar added in 2016. The focus is very much on producing perfect grapes and "wines of character" without fanfare.

 **Cornalin:** Some of the Mercier wines can be purchased only in small quantities, so great is the demand for these specialty wines with top reputations but small productions. Cornalin is a wine that ages beautifully when well made, and the Mercier's is considered one of the best. The wine is part of the Mémoire des Vins Suisses wines treasured for their aging capacity.

## ADDRESS

**Cave Mercier**
Crêt-Goubing 42
3960 Sierre
Tel: 027 455 4710
info@denismercier.ch
madeleine@denismercier.ch
denismercier.ch

## WINERY FEES

No. Reservation recommended.

## WHERE ELSE TO FIND THIS CELLAR'S WINES NEARBY

**L'Atelier Gourmand Didier de Courten**, Rue du Bourg 1, 3960 Sierre
027 455 13 51
info@hotel-terminus.ch
**Château De Villa**, Rue Sainte-Catherine 4, 3960 Sierre,
027 455 18 96
info@chateaudevilla.ch

# SIERRE MURAZ

## HEIGHTS ABOVE THE VINES AND SAVED GRAPES

CENTRAL VALAIS

| ▷··· STARTING POINT | ···✕ DESTINATION |
|---|---|
| **COLOMBIRE HAMLET** | **CAVE MAURICE ZUFFEREY, MURAZ-SIERRE** |

| SEASON | HIKE TYPE |
|---|---|
| **APRIL TO NOVEMBER** | **MODERATE /DIFFICULT**   |

| MAP REFERENCE | ⊙ DURATION |
|---|---|
| **SHEET 273T** | **3H 45M** |
| | ↦ LENGTH |
| | **12.3 KM** |

| 🔍 INTERESTING SIGHTS | |
|---|---|
| COLOMBIRE OUTDOOR HISTORICAL/CHEESE MUSEUM. BISSE DU TSITTORRET. CAVE DU SCEX MARKET/CAFÉ. MEDIEVAL VILLAGES OF VENTHÔNE/ANCHETTES. | ╱ CLIMB / DESCENT |
| | **186 M / 1,378 M** |

## CORNALIN
CAVE MAURICE ZUFFEREY

 RED

 COMPLEX, FRUITY, SOME COFFEE, SUBTLE HINTS OF CINNAMON

 BLACK CHERRIES, VERY ELEGANT TANNINS, WONDERFUL STRUCTURE AND DEPTH

 DRY, STILL

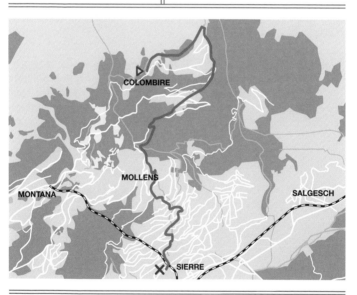

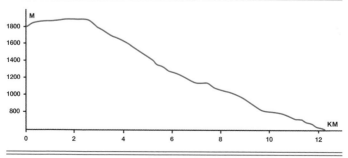

# DESCRIPTION OF THE ROUTE

Colombire to the Scex waterfall, along the Tsittorret Bisse (irrigation canal), is a popular family walk, especially pleasant with its shade and cool stream on a hot summer day. The first 45 minutes of the trail go uphill so gently that you don't notice you're climbing. At the Scex outdoor stand (in season), and restaurant (expect cheese and mountain air dried meats), the trail splits with a fine climb to a cirque left and above, and the long descent to the right. Waterways appear and disappear the length of the trail. This is part of an ancient cowherding path. These open fields are the old communal pastures for Mollens, historically a commune far larger than the village below which carries its name.

Partway down to Aminona, a peaceful stone and wood contemporary chapel sits atop a hill, just a few metres off the trail. The views are fine: the Matterhorn is visible on clear days. Continue down, following signs for Aminona, which is a collection of mostly modern chalets and three white towers, rather than a village. The 1960s plan was to build more than 20 of these towers, before mountain communes established zoning laws and restrictions.

Several paths separate and the threads often join each other again, so it's easy to take a wrong turn: follow signs for Aminona, then Mollens. The trail joins the road briefly before veering off to the left to run just above the small but powerful Sinièse River, which you hear but rarely glimpse. Mollens is a typical mountain farm village, or once was; the

central plaza was crowded with houses until a fire some decades ago razed most of them. There are two ways down to the church of St. Maurice-de-Laques; take the path to the left from the old center down a steep, open street where you can easily see the church. From there follow the yellow hiking trail signs for steep but handy shortcuts that avoid the many loops in the Route de Montana.

The top end of Venthône is mostly vines, grown here for wine for at least a millennia. From these it's a short winding walk to the left to the medieval village showing off a fortified 12th century castle and tower. Head down towards the Anchettes castle, built between the 14th and 17th centuries, with a side chapel built in 1649. Take the steps next to the chapel, following the signs for a picnic spot, the perfect place for a pause with a view. From here the trail hugs a wall (downhill then left towards a bisse and small waterfall and a patch of woodland). This is vineyard country par excellence, including some of Maurice Zufferey's vines. Carry on until you reach the houses in Muraz, turn right onto the village's one real street and walk until the road begins to descend to Sierre. The winery is on the left.

**Return**
Fifteen-minute walk to the Sierre train station.

**Notes**
This is a relatively easy hike for the entire length, but it is a steady downhill three-hour march after the first 45 minutes.

The hike starts at Colombire hamlet and cheese museum free shuttle bus stop. The bus runs through the middle of Crans-Montana and can be picked up in several places, including the funicular that runs between the resort and Sierre.

# CAVE MAURICE ZUFFEREY

Maurice Zufferey is widely considered to have one of the finest Cornalin wines anywhere, but a word of caution: this is a very difficult grape to grow and in some years the amount produced is very small. He, along with a couple of friends in the area, did much to save this grape from extinction but you have to pull the story out of him. He is a quiet, self-effacing, gentle man who spends any spare time he finds high in the mountains above Sierre where he grew up. His understanding of terroir is exceptional and his wines sing of it. Today he's training his son Adrien in the family winemaking arts.

**Cornalin:** Often considered the signature red Valais wine, this is the rare one from old vines. It ages very well.

## ADDRESS

**Cave Maurice Zufferey**
Chemin des Moulins 52
CH - 3960 Sierre
Tel: 027 455 4716
Cell: 079 204 4816
contact@mauricezufferey.ch
mauricezufferey.ch

## WINERY FEES

No. Limited regular hours or by appointment.

## WHERE ELSE TO FIND THIS CELLAR'S WINES NEARBY

**La Contrée**, Rue de la Vanire 1, 3960 Muraz,
27 455 12 91
lacontree@lacontree.ch
**Château De Villa**, Rue Sainte-Catherine 4, 3960 Sierre,
027 455 18 96
info@chateaudevilla.ch

# VENTHÔNE

## HIGH AND DRY, THEN COOL ACTIVE *BISSE*

CENTRAL VALAIS

| ▷⋯ STARTING POINT | ⋯✕ DESTINATION |
|---|---|
| **VEYRAS, MUZOT BUS STOP** | **CAVE MABILLARD-FUCHS, VENTHÔNE** |

| 🗓 SEASON | 🏁 HIKE TYPE |
|---|---|
| **APRIL TO NOVEMBER** IN DRY WEATHER | **DIFFICULT** |

| ⛰ MAP REFERENCE | ⏱ DURATION |
|---|---|
| **SHEET 273T** | **3H 45M** |

| | ↦ LENGTH |
|---|---|
| | **10.3 KM** |

| 🔍 INTERESTING SIGHTS | 〰 CLIMB / DESCENT |
|---|---|
| RAINER MARIA RILKE CHAPEL IN MIÈGE. MEDIEVAL HIGH VILLAGE OF CORDONA. RASPILLE RIVER LANGUAGE LINE. BISSE NEUF. | **653 M / 457 M** |

# HUMAGNE ROUGE
### CAVE MABILLARD-FUCHS

 RED

 VIOLETS,
WILD BERRIES,
SPICES

 PLEASINGLY SMOOTH,
SILKY TANNINS

 DRY,
STILL

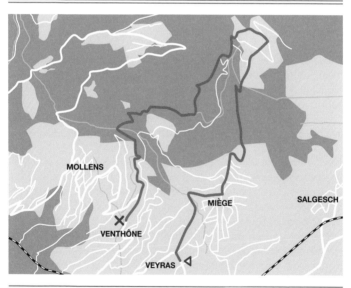

MOLLENS

MIÈGE

SALGESCH

✕
VENTHÔNE

VEYRAS ◁

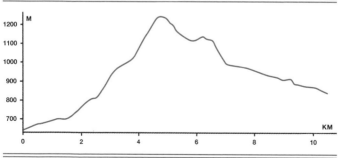

# DESCRIPTION OF THE ROUTE

This route will give the heart and legs a workout, despite being just over 10 km, with several stretches of very steep grade and slippery gravel underfoot.

The Muzot bus stop in Veyras, the trail starting point, offers a mini-dose of culture, for the Rainer Maria Rilke Culture Trail crosses here. Information panels on the Route de Miège recount the work of this famous German language poet. The route along Route du Moulin takes you through the old part of the village of Miège; at the modern church take a left: this is where the climb begins on small paved roads up through new homes and the top of the vines in Miège, at 980 m, until the edge of the Finges forest, or Pfynwald. The path is relatively easy to follow.

The initial forest walk – in one of Switzerland's three national Nature Parks – features low pine trees and scrub. On a sunny day this part of the trail is hot. Cordona, a handful of chalets at 1,240 m, is closer to streams and the trees are taller with welcome shade. From here to the *bisse* (irrigation canal) below, there are no benches and no drinking water, despite numerous fountains (used for animals).

Cordona was, in the Middle Ages, an important small village that belonged to the Seigneurs in Sion, with locals paying tithes on the farmland. The chapel and bourgeoisie house in this beautifully situated hamlet are the two oldest buildings and worth taking a moment to view. Cordona is technically part of Crans-Montana, but as an enclave, and it is the only residential area on the left bank of the Raspille River.

Follow hiking trail signs through the lower end of the collection of houses and walk towards the great face of the ravine wall that rises above the La Pauja river. The trail starts to head downhill. The first part is very pleasant, meadows and wildflowers in summer and babbling brooks – water is ever-present. Cross La Pauja on boards that serve as bridges to join the Miège-Cordona road, which has very little traffic. A bridge now crosses the river again as the water gains strength. Signage to leave the road is clear and here begins another rough stretch, steep and scrabbly underfoot. One such drop ends suddenly at the bisse walk, well-kept, and from here on, offering a gentle altitude change. It makes a big loop around the Sinièse river. There are two signs for Venthône. Be sure to take the right turn to get off the trail. The other trail option to the left goes down to the town park and playground, and comes out well below the winery. Once off the bisse trail, follow the main road; cross over to the gas station to the downhill sidewalk. Venthône is a medieval town; explore it by taking an underpass shortly after the winery.

**Return**
The stop for the bus that serves Sierre train station-Crans-Montana via Mollens is a two-minute walk from the winery.

# CAVE MABILLARD-FUCHS

Very reasonably priced and excellent wines from Madeleine and Jean-Yves Mabillard Fuchs (their son recently joined them), who have been working, with a focus on terroir, grape varieties and sustainability, and without much fanfare since they opened in 1993. Their vineyards are in a swath from Sierre to Venthône. Ask about wildlife and wild plants in their vineyards. The wines are notable for their aromatic purity.

 **Humagne Rouge:** Humagne Rouge has a reputation as the wine to drink with game. Like France's Beaujolais Nouveau, the product has suffered from harvest-time popularity with too many wines made with underripe grapes. This is one of the finer examples to cherish.

## ADDRESS

**Mabillard-Fuchs**
Route de Montana 18
3973 Venthône
Tel: 027 455 34 76
mabillard-fuchs@bluewin.ch
mabillard-fuchs.ch

## WINERY FEES

No

## WHERE ELSE TO FIND THIS CELLAR'S WINES NEARBY

**L'Atelier Gourmand Didier de Courten**, Rue du Bourg 1, 3960 Sierre
027 455 13 51
info@hotel-terminus.ch
**Château De Villa**, Rue Sainte-Catherine 4, 3960 Sierre,
027 455 18 96
info@chateaudevilla.ch

# SALGESCH

## NATURE REIGNS, MOUNTAIN PEOPLE BRIDGE THEIR GAP

UPPER VALAIS

| ▷⋯ STARTING POINT | ⋯✗ DESTINATION |
|---|---|
| **SIERRE-VISSOIE BUS LINE:** SIERRE-PARC DE FINGES BUS STOP | **CAVE DU RHODAN, SALGESCH** |
| 📅 SEASON | 🎋 HIKE TYPE |
| **MAY TO NOVEMBER** OR MID-WINTER (CHECK ICE AND SNOW CONDITIONS WITH THE PARK OFFICE) | **MODERATE** 🚶 |
| ⛰ MAP REFERENCE | ⏱ DURATION |
| **SHEET 273T** | **6H 15M** (WINTER ALTERNATIVE WITHOUT THE BHUTAN BRIDGE IS 3 HOURS) |
| | ↦ LENGTH |
| 🔍 INTERESTING SIGHTS | **22.6 KM** (APPROXIMATELY 15 KM WITHOUT THE BHUTAN BRIDGE LOOP) |
| PFYN NATURE PARK SWAMPS. BHUTAN SUSPENSION BRIDGE. PANORAMA AT VAREN CHURCH. OLD CHAPEL (KAPPÄLUHUBIL) TRAIL IN SALGESCH. | 〰 CLIMB / DESCENT |
| | **795 M / 757 M** |

## PINOT CUVÉE
## ESPACE BIO
### CAVE DU RHODAN

 RED

 BERRIES

 BERRIES AGAIN
(HARMONIOUS),
CLEAN, WELL-STRUCTURED

 DRY,
STILL

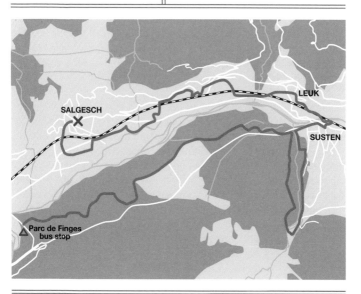

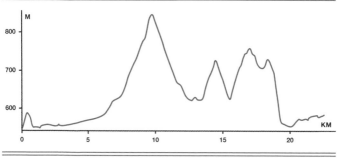

# DESCRIPTION OF THE ROUTE

The bus stop in Sierre, near the East Sierre autoroute exit, is right next to the entrance to the park. The path is well marked "Etangs" and easy to follow, as are all trails in this well-managed park. Continue towards the area of small marshes, which are home to many small animals and birds. The trail initially goes through woodland, but comes to an open meadow fairly soon.

At the end of the meadow, cross a small marshland bridge and follow the trail as it heads right. From this point, on the trail runs mostly parallel to the Rhone and, for some time, on the edge of woodland and brush, with cultivated fields just to the right. Cross a small farm road. The trail continues through scrub and pine forest, always close to farmland; follow signs for Susten and the Bhutan bridge. Cross over a canal that carries water from the Rhone downstream to a hydroelectric station in Chippis, next to Sierre.

Shortly after the canal, the hiking trail splits in two, both of which lead to the Bhutan bridge. The right-hand path, which the trail follows, crosses the busy road and goes directly to a housing area. Turn right following signs for the bridge and walk gently uphill for about 3 km. Shortly before the bridge the trail comes to a T-junction; take the left-hand path which skirts an open space briefly, then bends sharp right and continues through more pine forest to the bridge.

Cross over and walk back along the marked trail, where houses and small farms soon appear, to the village of Susten. The trail turns left soon before the Rhone, then right, simply to avoid the middle of town. The best place to cross this busy series of roundabouts, highways and bridges is from the small Susten central shopping area just above the highway down to the Leuk train station, following signs for the Bahnhof. Go through the train station parking lot to the small bridge and across the river, then begin to head uphill to Leuk Stadt. Stay on Alter Kehr and cross Leukerstrasse, but staying on the marked footpaths for Varen. The trail joins, leaves and rejoins streets several times. Turn left at Varengasse. The trail crosses the busy Umfahrungsstrasse, which is the main road to the resort of Leukerbad.

On the other side of this road follow the footpath along Hammerschmiede. The trail continues on this street as it heads back downhill to the lower bridge across the Dala River; an optional route that avoids dropping 100 meters and climbing back up is to take the larger, modern bridge above, rather than taking the left turn at Hammerschmiede, but this is the Leuk-Varen-Salgesch road and can be busy. Once across the lower bridge, stay on this street to climb up through the vines (take the right-hand option at the first junction) and into the hilly old village of Varen, crossing the main road from the Leuk upper bridge. The trail leads through the center of the village and then back down to the main road to Pfarrkirche Maria Sieben Schmerzen, a church with a fine panoramic view of the Rhone.

From here head west, away from the village for a moment, then follow the trail that leads downhill to Salgesch – there are several parallel trails along vineyard paths above and below the road, so stay on the marked path, which is parallel to the road but about 25 meters below it. It ends back at the road but soon after follows the marked trail that splits off to the left to head down again through the vineyards. It follows a rocky area, crosses the lower Leuk-Salgesch road and continues downhill. More vineyards, some wooded areas, more houses and barns – stay on the marked path to Salgesch. When the trail comes out of the woods it turns left at an old house and follows a small road towards the town. Go uphill and past a small group of modern apartments: at the roundabout take the first left, which leads past the train station.

Continue straight but instead of taking the underpass street that bends right, turn left onto Larschästrasse. After a small parking area on the left, the street becomes an agricultural road and after a few metres signposts appear on the right for the path around the Kapälluhubil. The pretty little chapel is on the hilltop and the path leads around it to the bottom end of Salgesch. Cross over the main street, Unterdorfstrasse, and head into town, but turn left at Foschastrasse, which twists and turns and climbs uphill. Follow signs for Cave du Rhodan.

**Return**
Seven-minute walk to the post office in the town square for a bus and 15-minute walk to the Salgesch train station.

**Notes**
The town of Salgesch is primarily German-speaking, but it is right on the language divide and thus is also known as Salquenen. The wines here are more generally called Salquenen.

The Pfyn Nature Park was created in 2005 with the concept that sections of wilderness and settled areas, residential and industrial, can share space and work together. The main office and information center is in the center of Salgesch, as is the Valais vine and wine museum. Pfyn/Finges is one of three regional parks "of national importance" and stretches from the Rhone, at 500 m a.s.l. to the Weisshorn, at 4,500 m a.s.l.

Pfynwald, inside the park, is a rare Mediterranean pine forest in the Alps built on glacial debris. The park is a biodiversity haven, with very dry rocky steppes, swamps near the Rhone, glacial streams that feed into the Rhone and a hydroelectric system canal. Volunteers from the communes who are members of the park work on cleanup and other projects throughout the year. Farmers have a number of biodiversity projects, including raising unusual breeds that hikers may come across, such as the ancient Galloway small white cows. It's a natural-ist's dream walk in summer, given the flora and fauna. Insect repellent is highly recommended.

The park is also an association of communes, with businesses and associations encouraged to become partners. It has more than 80 win-eries within its boundaries, 30 of them in Salgesch. The park's regional product label serves as a sustainable practices certification; 36-plus wines (and more are in the pipeline) are certified and products from 26 artisans are sold in small shops and supermarkets.

The entire trail can be followed year-round. Much of the park receives very little direct sunlight in winter, creating magical hoar-frost scenes, especially around the swampy areas. The higher land around the Bhutan bridge can become icy and snowy some of the winter and the marshy area waterlogged in spring, so it's important to check with the park office if the entire route is feasible. It's very easy to simply delete the loop to the Bhutan bridge at Susten and continue directly to Varen on the other side of the Rhone, cutting the trip by about two hours. This colourful 134-meter suspension cable bridge with its Bhutanese prayer flags crosses the wild (occasionally torrential) Illgraben at a height of 80 m. It was opened in 2004, a joint Swiss–Bhutan project.

The small chapel loop in Salgesch can also be easily skipped; simply head for the middle of town from the train station and follow signs up to the winery, which is on the western edge of Salgesch.

# CAVE DU RHODAN

One member of this large family instigated the town's decision to create Switzerland's first AOC (appellation d'origine contrôlée) in 1988, after quality levels had dipped during a wine boom phase that led to overproduction in much of Europe. The family was one of the first in Switzerland to move to biodynamic winemaking, convinced that sustainable practices were the only way to ensure quality. Olivier and Sandra Mounir took charge of the family winery in 2007 and have continued to build its reputation for pioneering work around sustainable practices – with a new winery in 2017 and adding sheep in the vineyard that nibble near a solar research project which could have international implications for making vineyard land use more efficient.

The family's reputation for excellence goes back at least to winning the world wine award in 1972 just 10 years after the Cave du Rhodan was created, for the best red wine of the competition, a Pinot Noir. Today, new disease-resistant grapes have joined their organic and biodynamic wines.

 **Pinot Cuvée Espace Bio:** This is a classic Pinot, very well made, the first wine from Cave du Rhodan to earn the Swiss organic label. It is one of a trio of wines labelled "Espace" from grapes grown on the Trong terroir, which are certified by the Pfyn Nature Park. Trong is worked according to biodynamic principles and the focus is strongly on preserving the quality of the soil. The wines ferment spontaneously in concrete eggs.

## ADDRESS

**Cave du Rhodan – Mounir Weine**
Flantheystr. 1
3970 Salgesch
Tel: 027 455 04 07
mounir@rhodan.ch
rhodan.ch

## WINERY FEES

CHF10–17 plus additional options.
Regular hours.

## WHERE ELSE TO FIND THIS CELLAR'S WINES NEARBY

**Le Cercle d'Or**, Schafgasse 2, 3970 Salgesch,
079 882 95 95
**Hôtel de la Poste**, Rue du Bourg 22, 3960 Sierre,
027 456 57 60
info@hotel-sierre.ch

# LEUK

## OH FOR THE LOVE OF RYE! AND PRECIOUS BONES

UPPER VALAIS

| ▷··· STARTING POINT | ···✕ DESTINATION |
|---|---|
| **BRATSCH DORF BUS STOP (FROM LEUK TRAIN STATION)** | **VIN D'ŒUVRE, LEUK** |

| 📅 SEASON | 🗺 HIKE TYPE |
|---|---|
| **APRIL TO NOVEMBER** | **DIFFICULT** |

| 🗺 MAP REFERENCE | ⏱ DURATION |
|---|---|
| **SHEET 273T** | **3H** |

| | ↦ LENGTH |
|---|---|
| | **9.6 KM** |

| 🔍 INTERESTING SIGHTS | ∿ CLIMB / DESCENT |
|---|---|
| ERSCHMATT: VALAIS RYE BREAD CENTER. EXPERIMENTAL BOTANICAL GARDEN. SWISS ROCKY STEPPES. HOHE BRÜCKE. LEUK: BEINHAUS (OSSUARY), MEDIEVAL CASTLE. | **384 M / 757 M** |

## TO DIE FOR
VIN D'OEUVRE

| | |
|---|---|
| 👁 | RED |
| 👃 | FRUITY, NOTABLY DEEPLY RIPE STRAWBERRIES |
| 👅 | FRESH, FRUITY, SMOOTH, GOOD TANNINS, BALANCE |
| 🍷 | DRY, STILL |

GAMAY

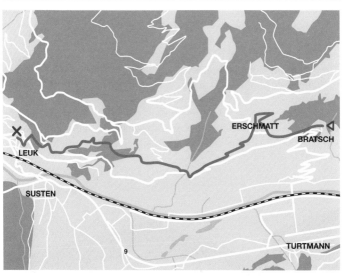

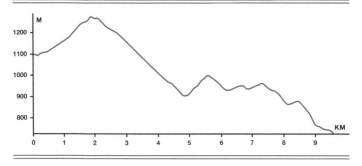

# DESCRIPTION OF THE ROUTE

The bus from the Leuk train station stops in Erschmatt before Bratsch, and it is possible to get out there and cut the hike a bit shorter. But Bratsch, which is 150 m lower than Erschmatt, sits on the edge of the forest, and starting the trail here improves understanding of what the rocky steppes of the Swiss Alps are all about. From the Bratsch bus stop follow Dorfstrasse uphill. It becomes Bienen, then Mühledorf; where the road splits, take Kummen up the hill. Follow this road along the edge of the forested area and into the village of Erschmatt, where the street is also known as Hauptstrasse. Continue on what is first called Kummenstrasse, then Kummenweg to the center and at the main plaza head to the right and uphill on Oberdorf (note that street names are confusing here, with several having the same or similar names), following signs for the botanical garden, Sortengarten Erschmatt.

The trail continues after a stop here, along the top end of the village on Hugosteinstrasse, where the open steppes are clearly visible: Turn left at Oberer Schleif, continue straight to Dorfplatz, turn right and immediately left onto Kreuzstrasse. When the street ends, turn left and immediately right onto the marked trail, following signs from here for Hohe Brücke and Leuk Stadt.

The trail down to the bridge descends steadily across windswept open rock and fields, much of it wild, with fine views of the mountains and the Rhone below – and no shade. The path is roughly parallel to the Erschmatt-Leuk road below, and joins it briefly just before the bridge. While the road follows the new bridge, hikers can happily cross over the 16th century bridge and visit the tiny chapel.

From here the marked footpath climbs to the hamlet of Oberrotafu; where the trail splits, take the higher path through the top end of this collection of houses. Stay on the trail until it joins the small Brunnen road and continue on it as it turns right and becomes Obere Lichten. The road bends left and soon after there is a marked trail to the right; take this path. When it splits, take the higher road to the right. Continue on this path, which heads to the large Swisscom satellite dishes and the site of the forest that burned in 2003. Before reaching them the trail turns right and loops back left, joining Brentjongweg, a path that heads around the bottom of the satellite dishes, turning left to go downhill through vineyards to Badnerstrasse.

Turn right onto the road and stay on it until a second footpath option to the left appears, marked Kreuzweg. Follow this until the trail markers point left to Leuk; the trail leads down to the cemetery and the main Leuk-Leukerbad road. Cross the road to the village and head straight downhill to visit the remarkable 20 meter-long wall of skulls at the charnel house, Beinhaus, in a chapel on the side of St. Stephan church. Then take the first right below the church, Eihorugässi, and follow it as it bends right. At the intersection of Gintig, take that street down a short but steep hill and the winery is on the left.

**Return**
Ten-minute walk downhill to the Leuk Stadt train station.

**Notes**
Erschmatt was and is again a Valais rye bread center with a bakery that gives bread baking lessons. For centuries these high steppes have been an important grain and cereal center for the region, in particular for growing the rye that goes into the bread so famous as part of every Swiss Valais Platter of dried meats and cheeses. Linked to this history is the Erschmatt steppes research and experimental botanical garden (cereals, grasses, wild plants).

The 16th century Hohe Brücke arched bridge, 100 m above the Feschelbach, is a wonder of medieval construction and the gorge that appears to have no bottom is equally impressive.

Leuk is the site of one of Switzerland's largest-ever forest fires (August 2003), above the town. The arsonist responsible, later jailed and given psychiatric treatment for setting 36 other fires, destroyed more than 300 hectares of forest. The fire broke out next to Swisscom's large satellite dishes above Leuk Stadt and roared uphill in just minutes. Two decades later, the regeneration of the forest is the focus of a long-term research programme that is bearing fruit (happily, even literally).

The vertically oriented town of Leuk is a treasure chest of architectural interest, with some curiosities: the Beinhaus (ossuary) walls of skulls are not as sinister as they first seem. This is where the dead for whom there was no room in the cemetery were placed on holy ground. Leuk medieval castle topped its restoration with a startling glass cupola by architect Mario Botta; the medieval old town has a charming mix of buildings.

# VIN D'OEUVRE

Isabella and Stéphane Kellenberger are from Bern but decided to grow grapes and set up their winery in Valais in 2012. They have vines in Fully, Raron, Visperterminen and Leuk, some 75 km apart with vineyards in each location that are some of the country's highest. Given the already daunting workload and their strong commitment to sustainability, the storm destruction in 2017 of two-thirds of the high vines, terraces and sustaining wall in Raron, and the subsequent renovation of this ancient vineyard, is an indication of the energy they pour into this winery. Isabella's background in marketing shows, starting with names – the play on words for the winery name and catchy wine names in English (Love never dies, Born to be wild). She has organized hiking packages, development of a barrels "godparents" program and their involvement in a number of outside projects. One of these is the village's Cornalin Vitis Antiqua 1798 wine, a joint project by five wineries from the grapes of a Cornalin vine that is the country's oldest vine and its carefully reproduced offspring.

 **To Die For:** This is a very classy Gamay, elegant and yet a fun crowd-pleaser, a wine that in 2013 was named the best overall red at the national competition Grand Prix du Vin Suisse, bringing the attention of the wine world to this young couple. The grapes are grown in Fully in lower Valais.

## ADDRESS

**Vin d'oeuvre**
Gintig 4
3953 Loèche-Ville
Tel: 027 473 3838 / 079 793 3787
info@vindoeuvre.ch
vindoeuvre.ch

## WINERY FEES

CHF15–22 with various options.

## WHERE ELSE TO FIND THIS CELLAR'S WINES NEARBY

**Restaurant Taverne**, Friedhofstrasse 2, 3952 Susten,
027 473 18 77
loretan.marco@gmail.com
**Relais Bayard**, Kantonsstrasse 151, 3952 Susten,
027 474 96 96
info@relaisbayard.ch

# RARON

## GERMAN POET TO CAVE CHURCH

UPPER VALAIS

| ▷⋯ STARTING POINT | ⋯✕ DESTINATION |
|---|---|
| **AUSSERBERG, HAUPTBAHNHOF BUS STOP** | **WEINGUT CIPOLLA, RARON BOURG** |

 SEASON

**YEAR-ROUND UNLESS SNOW**

 HIKE TYPE

**EASY**

 MAP REFERENCE

**274T**

🕐 DURATION

**2H 45M**

↦ LENGTH

**10.9 KM**

🔍 INTERESTING SIGHTS

POET RAINER MARIA RILKE'S BURIAL PLACE.
EUROPE'S LARGEST CAVE CHURCH.
UNESCO SITE WITH MEDIEVAL KNIGHT WOODEN
STATUES.

〜 CLIMB / DESCENT

**632 M / 1,008 M**

## HEIDA TOLI
### WEINGUT CIPOLLA

 WHITE

 COMPLEX WITH CITRUS,
EXOTIC FRUITS,
ESPECIALLY LYCHEE,
SOME PINEAPPLE

 RICH,
ROUND,
LIVELY

 DRY,
STILL

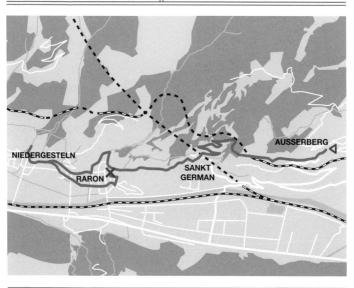

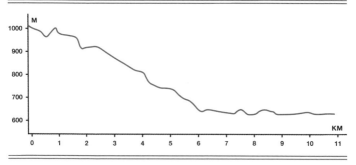

# DESCRIPTION OF THE ROUTE

Take the postal bus from Visp, which is a far better option than driving on the steep and narrow hairpin bends road. The town center of Ausserberg is up the road from the Hauptbahnhof bus stop. From the bus stop walk downhill to the yellow trail arrows that point to Sankt German and Raron. This begins with a short, very steep farm vehicles' road that quickly smooths out to a bucolic walk through woods and open stretches. The surface switches from paved to gravel to grassy and back; the steepest bits have been built with a kindly blend of pebbles and large stones.

Continue on this path to Sankt German – there are no real alternatives. This north side of the Rhone rises steeply and offers spectacular views of farmland, a fast-moving young Rhone and groups of peaks on the far side. The first half of the hike is through shaded patches of woodland. Wild fields mixed with rugged dry rock land rise to the right.

The first vines signal that Sankt German is near, followed shortly by an explanatory panel, in German, about the village's history as the wine town of the region. The path dips down and past a small *bisse*, one of hundreds of ancient irrigation channels in Valais that carry water from the glaciers to farmland below. This one rushes through a paved ditch on the right: the payoff is to look back and see it continue along an elegant old wooden airborne trough to maintain the steady 1% fall that makes the bisses so efficient.

In Sankt German, carry on straight along Dorfstrasse and continue on this street out of town (vineyards suddenly appear everywhere) to the Burgkirche high above Raron.

A feature of this walk is the frequency of benches for snapshot and panoramic views. Another is the number of churches, chapels and crosses in this traditional stronghold of Catholicism. The rugged little white St. Anna Kapelle built into a rocky slab with cactus plants in its crevices is just after Sankt German. The doors are generally unlocked. Respectful visitors are welcome, but are asked to close the doors tightly to keep the eternal votive candles lit.

Nearby are drystone walls. Valais has more than 3,000 km of terraced vineyards with drystone walls, some of which go back centuries. Maintaining these is a time-consuming, arduous and costly task, but they are considered effective as well as being a part of the canton's heritage.

At the landmark Raron Burgkirche, before heading down a steep paved walk to the old town, take a short detour to the church. It is famous as the burial place of Rainer Maria Rilke, an important early 20th century German language lyrical poet who lived in the region. The church also offers spectacular (windy!) views and a local graveyard with photos of the deceased.

Continue on the same path – there are no alternatives – then go right at Stalde, to Oberdorfgasse, through the upper old town. Veer right

towards the Bietsch river: there's a waterfall to the right and 900-meter high vineyards, including the Toli vine parcel, home to Romain Cipolla's Heida grapes, which makes it clear why making wine here has never been easy. Turn left and walk along the Bietschiweg to the site of the massive rockfall of winter 2021, which has since been dynamited to stabilise the rock.

Turn right and follow Stadelmattenstrasse/Obergeschstrasse/Wannu-moosstrasse into Niedergesteln village, part of the UNESCO Jungfrau-Aletsch site. Just above it are the Gesteln 12th century castle ruins with wooden knights leading up to it. Turn right at Dorfstrasse. Follow signs and Oberdorfstrasse to Jolischlucht, a fine viewing point. Retrace the trail to Wannutrogstrasse and take the right fork along a patch of mixed farmland and small industry to Raron center and St. Michael's church.

The winery itself often has no sign out front and little indication that there is a cellar here; it's open by appointment.

**Return**
It's a 10-minute walk to the Raron regional line train station.

**Notes**
The postal bus ride's view heading up to Ausserberg is distracting, and the stop is easily overlooked – buzz the overhead button for Hauptbahn-hof, as this is an optional stop for what is a bit of a misnomer, just a roadside pullover.

St. Michael's is Europe's largest church built (1974) entirely inside a rock. It sits directly under the Burgkirche, which is at the top of the cliff, its contemporary lines and large bells in stark contrast to Rilke's resting place. Even those who usually prefer to skip visiting churches will find this one intriguing, with its high vaulted natural rock ceiling.

# WEINGUT CIPOLLA

Romain Cipolla is a one-man wonder, a young vigneron from Fribourg whose family is not in the wine business; with mother-tongue French, he settled in the region of Upper Valais German dialect-speakers in order to work old and difficult, often high vineyards, some of them on the verge of being abandoned. He makes a startling number of wines, all of them very good, but his Heida Toli (called Paien rather than Heida from Sierre downriver), is a wine of great character, from the vines you see at the top of the cirque above the town – daunting, steep slopes at 900 meters. He's mostly out in his vineyards, which are in several villages, or in the cellar in Sankt German making wine or delivering to restaurants throughout the region, so be sure to contact him ahead of time.

**Heida Toli:** high acidity, will age well with secondary aromas, great character.

## ADDRESS

**Weingut Cipolla**
Unterdorf 11
3942 Raron
Tel: 079 201 8131
info@weingut-cipolla.ch
weingut-cipolla.ch

## WINERY FEES

No. Reservation only.

## WHERE ELSE TO FIND THIS CELLAR'S WINES NEARBY

Recent restaurant ownership changes mean this is uncertain as the book goes to press; contact Romain Cipolla.

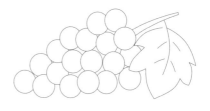

# VISPERTERMINEN

## GETTING SOME HEIGHT, HEIDA TOP WINES, HIGHEST VINES

© HEIDADORF

UPPER VALAIS

| ▷⋯ STARTING POINT | ⋯✕ DESTINATION |
|---|---|
| **TOP OF THE GIW CHAIRLIFT IN HEIDADORF (VISPERTERMINEN)** | **ST. JODERN KELLEREI, VISPERTERMINEN** |

| 📅 SEASON | 🔁 HIKE TYPE |
|---|---|
| **YEAR-ROUND** | **MODERATE** 🥾 |

| ⛰ MAP REFERENCE | 🕐 DURATION |
|---|---|
| **SHEET 274T** | **2H 20M** |

**├→ LENGTH**

**6.8 KM**

**🔍 INTERESTING SIGHTS**

VISPERTERMINEN'S OLD TOWN.
GEBIDUMSEE WITH VIEWS OF MATTERHORN.
UNTERSTALDEN TERRACED VINEYARDS.

**〜 CLIMB / DESCENT**

**419 M / 417 M**

## HEIDA GRAND CRU VISPERTERMINEN
### ST. JODERN KELLEREI

WHITE

NOTES OF HONEY,
CITRUS FRUITS,
EXOTIC FRUITS WITH HINTS OF
HAZELNUT AND DRIED FRUITS

FRESHNESS,
ROUND AND AMPLE,
GOOD ACIDITY, HARMONIOUS,
LONG IN MOUTH

DRY,
STILL

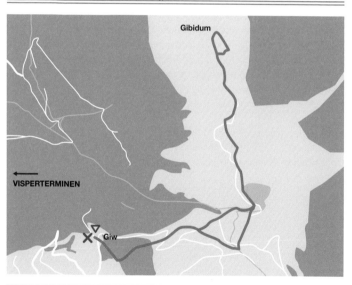

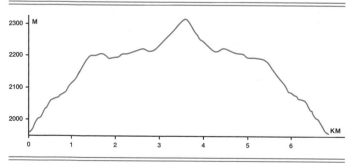

# DESCRIPTION OF THE ROUTE

From Heidadorf take the Sesselbahn Giw. At the top of the chairlift, go to the right of the T-bar which carries skiers further up the mountainside. This is one of the official Visperterminen snowshoe trails (Panoramaweg), so follow the yellow hiking markers that are complemented by purple snowshoe trail poles and signs.

The first part of the trail is a steep climb through trees to reach open areas. Signposts to follow: Panoramaweg to Bord, then Gebidumpass and Gebidumsee, Gebidum (the highest point on the trail). The trail turns left at a stream and runs alongside it; shortly after coming out above the tree line, the trail crosses another one: carry on straight but note that this is the point where the return trip loop rejoins and retraces the first part of the trail.

Continue until reaching the juncture of several trails and follow signposts left, towards the small lake. The edge of the lake is the point where the return trip will split off to go along the bottom edge of the bluffs. For now, bear left at the lake and continue straight, climbing gently to Gebidum. The trail makes a loop here, not quite reaching the ski lift area. After making the loop, retrace the hike to the lake, walking half the length of it before taking the trail that splits off to the right. Continue – it becomes a slightly larger trail – until the intersection with the path back down to Giw. Retrace steps to the top of the chairlift.

From here the trail goes down by way of the chairlift to avoid unpredictably slippery slopes (see notes), and from Heidadorf by bus down to Unterstalden (Kellerei stop).

© HEIDADORF

### Return

Kellerei is the name of the bus stop directly in front of the winery; buses run regularly between Heidadorf above and Visp (train station) below.

### Notes

Not a dog friendly hike (note: chairlift), but some trails up from Heidadorf allow dogs.

This is a hike that can be extended in summer; see notes below. Whatever the season, start by taking the chairlift from Heidadorf (the village of Visperterminen) to Giw, and begin the walk there. It's a circular walk that may require snowshoes, mainly for the steep slope at the start and finish.

The hike in winter is much slower than in summer with some sections (notably the departure point) steep and occasionally slippery. In summer it combines well with a walk down to the winery, an additional hour (3 km), following yellow arrow signposts for Unter Stalden. It is difficult to walk down to the winery from Heidadorf in winter because

several steep stretches are in the shade and remain icy much of the time. Thus the trail as described takes the chairlift down to Heidadorf and the bus down to Unter Stalden.

Whichever season: allow time to explore the very old village, winding hilly alleyways and the architecture of Heidadorf.

# ST. JODERN KELLEREI

Everything about this exceptional and impressive cooperative is surprising. It has the highest vines in continental Europe, at 1,150 m a.s.l. The large collection of almost secret south-facing vines just below the winery surely qualify as among the most spectacular and beautiful in the world. The vines are owned mostly by weekend growers with very small vineyards for whom their land and vines represent an attachment to strong local traditions. The cellar was renovated in 1980 and 120 coop members brought in their grapes, at a point when overproduction and falling grape prices were a problem throughout Switzerland. The winery struggled to raise both quality and its profile. In recent years its hard-earned success has encouraged these small growers/members – who now receive a better price for their grapes than most in Switzerland. By the 2020s more than 500 growers were selling their grapes to the cooperative, whose wines are reaping significant international and national awards. Despite producing some 400,000 "units" (bottles of varying sizes), many of the wines sell out quickly.

**Heida Grand Cru Visperterminen:** Heida is the upper Valais name for this wine, generally called Païen in central and lower Valais. The grape is known elsewhere as Traminer – not to be confused with Gewürztraminer, which is a mutation of this grape. The winery makes an impressive range of Heida wines, which are fun to compare during a tasting session. Heida Veritas, made according to a very old local style, is produced in small quantities and is the top of the line (the 2018 was named Best of Show at *Decanter* magazine's annual international awards). The Grand Cru is made in a contemporary style, as is the AOC Heida Veritas. The Grand Cru is new: officially launched in 2021, created to ensure an excellent quality modern wine and encourage members of this cooperative. The first vintage wine sold out in less than a month.

## ADDRESS

**St. Jodern Kellerei**
Unterstalden 2
3932 Visperterminen
Tel: 027 948 4348
info@jodernkellerei.ch
jodernkellerei.ch

## WINERY FEES

CHF15–33 for six wines plus options. The winery strongly encourages visits to the cellar, by appointment. Open during working hours M–S for tastings.

## WHERE ELSE TO FIND THIS CELLAR'S WINES NEARBY

**Spycher**, Kanzleiweg 40, 3932 Visperterminen,
027 946 71 59
**Bergrestaurant Giw**, Giw 1, 3932 Visperterminen,
027 946 36 48
info@bergrestaurant-giw.ch

# THREE LAKES

# MILVIGNES

## CLASS, ELEGANCE, CHARM: LAKE NEUCHATEL

NEUCHÂTEL

▷⋯ **STARTING POINT**

**BEVAIX TRAIN STATION**

⋯✗ **DESTINATION**

**CAVE CHAMBLEAU,**
CORMONDRÈCHE ABOVE COLOMBIER

📅 **SEASON**

**YEAR-ROUND**

🗺 **HIKE TYPE**

**EASY** 🚶

🗺 **MAP REFERENCE**

**SHEET 242T**

🕐 **DURATION**

**2H 40M**

↦ **LENGTH**

**10.35 KM**

🔍 **INTERESTING SIGHTS**

WATERFRONT VINEYARDS.
NEUCHÂTEL VINE AND WINE MUSEUM
(10-MINUTE DETOUR).
CHÂTEAU DE COLOMBIER: MILITARY MUSEUM.

〰 **CLIMB / DESCENT**

**148 M / 121 M**

### PUR SANG
CAVE CHAMBLEAU

PINOT NOIR

👁 RED

👃 COMPLEX,
RED FRUITS AND SPICES

👄 FRESH,
YET DEEP AND RICH

🍷 DRY,
STILL

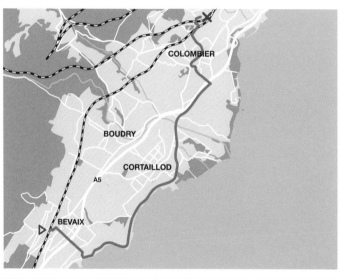

COLOMBIER

BOUDRY

CORTAILLOD

A5

BEVAIX

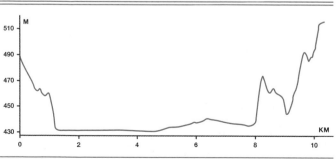

# DESCRIPTION OF THE ROUTE

From the train station in Bevaix, head north and then east along the Rue de la Gare in the direction of the lake. The street becomes Chemin des Près; continue along this street and just after the autoroute take the footpath to the right, which runs parallel to the street.

At the Chemin du Vignoble, the footpath rejoins Chemin de Basuges and continues towards the lake. Stay on this street until Chemin du Moulin; turn left and carry on along the waterfront.

The name of the street changes, but this path between the waterfront and a series of well-known vineyards – Vignes du Châtelard, Vignes de l'Abbaye – is one of canton Neuchatel's favourite walks. At the

Pointe du Grain, the pebbly beach offers a toe-cooling respite for summer hikers; the trail bends left here to continue along the waterfront with one Neuchatel notable terroir vineyard after another on the left. Continue along the lakeside to Petit Cortaillod, a small marina and a handful of houses. In the center take the hiking trail option to the right, through the parking area and along the street called Petit-Cortaillod at the end of it. At the Y-junction go left along Chemin de la Roussette through a small commercial and industrial zone until the street ends at Avenue François-Borel. Turn left and almost immediately turn right onto a footpath, Bas-de-Sachet, which leads to the Areuse river. Once across the river – the bridge accommodates cars, bike and pedestrians – take the first right, where a small road, Chemin de la Plaine, separates from the main road. It leads right and soon runs next to the railway with a relatively busy road next to that. The small Neuchatel airport is just on the right. Despite traffic, this is a pleasant and easy footpath.

Continue until the first intersection, Plaine d'Areuse, which has an overpass and stairs: go around the bottom of the stairs and turn left onto Chemin de Chenailleta. Continue on this street, past a cemetery on the right, until the street bends right and joins the start of

Creux-du-Sable to go into the old town. At the top of the street, at a T-junction, turn left onto Rue Basse, then right onto Rue Haute, and right again as Rue Haute continues in this direction. Turn left onto Rue du Vieux-Moulin, then take the second left onto Chemin du Pontet. At a four-way intersection turn left onto Chemin des Battieux and continue, climbing gently, to Route de la Traversière; continue on Chemin des Battieux, which briefly jogs left before a roundabout; stay on it after the roundabout. Shortly before the train tracks, turn right onto Chemin du Rosy.

The small road turns left at the railway underpass, then right briefly and left again to climb up towards the winery. Stay on the road rather than footpaths and go over another smaller train track. The first (and smaller) entrance to the winery is signposted on the right, where there are a couple of farm buildings just as the road bends to the left. Follow the little dirt road through vineyards to the winery, which is visible, ignoring signs for the main entrance, which is further up the road and to the right.

**Return**
Walk 20 minutes to the castle or the old town center to catch a bus.

**Notes**
The winery is a bit out of the way for anyone using public transport, but the trail is well worth the extra trouble. The lakeside walk is a treasure, followed by a complete change of scenery in the old village of Colombier and then the climb to the winery, which is everything you might hope to find in a Swiss winery (contemporary area for tanks, fine old cellar for maturing in wood). The walk is easy throughout.

# CAVE CHAMBLEAU

Lake Neuchatel is a beautiful lake and the winery, which is atop the hillside and set back from the lake, has one of the finest views around – its twin towers are also easily visible, dominating the heights here. The Burgat family bought the winery in 1950 and has built it into one of Switzerland's finest cellars. Louis-Philippe began moving towards organic winemaking in 2001. Since 2017 the entire domain has been organic and is known for a classy combination of elegant marketing, fine wines and pioneering efforts with organic wines.

 **Pur Sang:** It would be hard to overstate how remarkable this wine is. The 2018 vintage recently won *Falstaff* magazine's award for best Swiss Pinot Noir and the 2011 one was named by Mémoire des Vins Suisses as the best Swiss vintage (aged) wine of 2021, two impressive accolades from fellow professionals. It is one of three Pinot Noirs produced here, all of them fine wines, but this is the winery's selection of its best grapes, made slooooowly and matured in barrels for 12–18 months. A beauty, pure and simple.

## ADDRESS

**Domaine de Chambleau**
2013 Colombier NE
Tel: 032 731 16 66
info@chambleau.ch
chambleau.ch

## WINERY FEES

No. Regular hours.

## WHERE ELSE TO FIND THIS CELLAR'S WINES NEARBY

**Restaurant Robinson**, Rives du Lac 11, 2013 Milvignes,
032 545 32 32
info@robinson-restaurant.ch
**La Taverne du Château**, Rue du Château 1, 2013 Colombier,
032 845 02 00
**Brasserie du Poisson**, Rue des Epancheurs 1, 2012 Milvignes,
032 731 62 31
lepoisson-auv@bluewin.ch

# MÔTIER-VULLY

## LAKE MURTEN'S GORY GHOSTS, WATCHFUL TOWERS, TRANQUIL LANDSCAPE

© PIERRE CUONY PHOTOGRAPHIES

MURTEN/MORAT

 ▷⋯ STARTING POINT

**TRAIN STATION MURTEN AKA MORAT**

⋯✕ DESTINATION

**LE PETIT CHÂTEAU WINERY, MÔTIER**

 SEASON

**YEAR-ROUND**

HIKE TYPE

**EASY**

MAP REFERENCE

**SHEET 242T**

DURATION

**2H 45M**

LENGTH

**10.9 KM**

INTERESTING SIGHTS

MEDIEVAL CITY OF MURTEN WITH ITS MUSEUM.
BURGUNDIAN CANNONS.
VULLY PATRICIAN VIGNERON HOMES.
ST. PIERRE CHURCH.

CLIMB / DESCENT

**81 M / 94 M**

# FREIBURGER
## LE PETIT CHÂTEAU

WHITE

FRUITY — PINEAPPLE — AND SPICY

RICH, DEEP, MINERAL AND SALINE NOTES

DRY, STILL

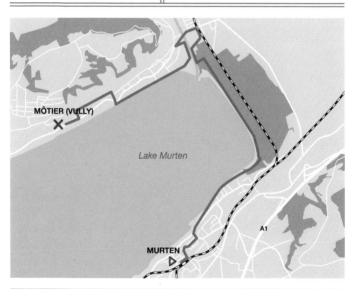

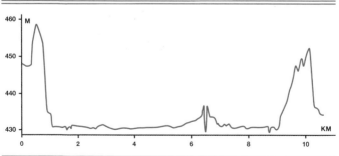

# DESCRIPTION OF THE ROUTE

The trail starts in front of the Murten (German)/Morat (French) train station. With the station behind, turn right on Bahnhofstrasse and left at the roundabout (still Bahnhofstrasse) and continue straight until the castle becomes visible (the museum is to the left just a few steps down Lausannestrasse). Go towards the old town from the Y-junction via Schlossgasse and turn left into the castle courtyard, overlooking the lake. Enter the old town by following Schlossgasse, which turns left and becomes Hauptgasse, the main street of the old part of the town. After wandering through the old town, return to Hauptgasse and go out through the walls to Bernstrasse and immediately head left along the footpath, also called Bernstrasse. Cross the main road and take the footpath to the waterfront. Here, the trail picks up Murten's famously busy and lovely boardwalk.

From this point to nearly the end of the trail, simply stay on the waterfront path as it bends around the lake. At Sugiez it takes a jog left, then right, then right and then left and left again in order to cross a bridge over the Canal de la Broye, which empties into the lake here. At the end of the bridge turn left to follow the canal and then right as the footpath again follows the lakefront.

At Praz the trail turns right to go through the village along Chemin du Ruisseau and slightly uphill to take Chemin du Péloset, a road parallel to the lake road but much less busy, with vineyards on both sides and views of the lake below. Continue until the steep little road Ruelle des Vaches; turn left to head downhill into Môtier. The trail goes down to the bottom and turns right onto Ruelle des Vignerons, which joins the Route du Lac, but the option to turn right earlier onto Ruelle du Vieux Moulin also works: it meets up with Ruelle des Vignerons. The winery is on the right shortly after the trail joins the Route du Lac, just before the Route du Débarcadère.

**Return**
There is bus service on the Route du Lac, a five minute walk.

**Notes**

This is an easy and entertaining walk. It's a good idea to include time to explore the town of Murten and learn about its history. Boat service on the lake in summer makes it easy to return here from Môtier. Morat/ Murten played a decisive role in the early history of the Swiss Confederation and for anyone with children at the age where gory history is interesting, it doesn't get much more thrilling than the 1476 Battle of Morat.

Mont Vully can be added for hikers who want more of a challenge and a chance to see the fine views of lakes and the Jura and Alps mountain ranges. Allow a good hour and 20 minutes to do the extra 4 km round-trip from Praz, the town next to Môtier (in the direction of Murten/ Morat), with a climb/descent of about 250 meters.

# LE PETIT CHÂTEAU

The Simonet family has been making wine for 200 years. At the turn of the century, Eric was a pioneer in the region for bringing in new grape varieties. Today the family has 16 hectares and some 20 grapes – it's the most recent generation with sons Fabrice and Stéphane who have put the family on a larger Swiss wine map, pushing into biodynamic production (the entire domain since 2016) from vineyard to bottle and promoting their work with a high level of marketing. The vines have been certified since 2019 by Demeter, the international biodynamic organization, as are the wines starting with the 2020 vintage. The Simonet brothers are also active members of the Junge Schweizer Neue Winzer group of under 40-year-old Swiss vignerons who pool their knowledge and resources as part of efforts to ensure the high quality of Swiss wines.

 **Freiburger:** One of the wines in which the Simonets take great pride, for it is a very rare grape in Switzerland. They make two versions of it. These are not wines that leave you indifferent and they can be quite exciting with, for example, Asian foods.

## ADDRESS

**Le Petit Château**
Route du Lac 134
1787 Môtier (Vully), Fribourg
Tel: 026 673 1493
info@lepetitchateau.ch
lepetitchateau.ch

## WINERY FEES

No. By appointment in winter or within summer hours.

## WHERE ELSE TO FIND THIS CELLAR'S WINES NEARBY

**Restaurant du Port**, Route du Lac 127, 1787 Môtier (Vully),
026 673 14 02
info@restaurantduport.ch

# TWANN

## A BRACELET OF AROMAS: LAKE BIEL/BIENNE, VERTIGINOUS VINES, CASCADES

BIEL/BIENNE

© HEINZ RINDLISBACHER

| ▷··· STARTING POINT | ···✕ DESTINATION |
|---|---|
| **NEUVEVILLE TRAIN STATION** | **SCHOTT WEINE TWANN** |
| 🗓 SEASON | 🎫 HIKE TYPE |
| **APRIL–NOVEMBER** | **MODERATE** 🚶 |
| ⛰ MAP REFERENCE | 🕐 DURATION |
| **SHEET 232T** | **2H 15M** |
| | ↦ LENGTH |
| 🔍 INTERESTING SIGHTS | **8.3 KM** |
| LAKE BIEL/BIENNE VINEYARDS. VIEWS OF ALPINE CHAIN. TWANNBACHSCHLUCHT (GORGES AND WATERFALLS). | ～ CLIMB / DESCENT |
| | **264 M / 263 M** |

**AROMA DER LANDSCHAFT**
**SAUVIGNON-ORANGE**
SCHOTT-WEINE

WHITE

THE BEST OF SAUVIGNON
— ALL THINGS GREEN,
HERBACEOUS — BECAUSE
THE WINERY IS GOOD AT
PICKING WHEN JUST RIPE

THE ACIDITY OF THIS GRAPE
IS THERE, AS IS THE SLIGHT
SOURNESS OR YEASTINESS
THAT CAN BE PART OF
NATURAL WINES

DRY,
STILL ORANGE WINE

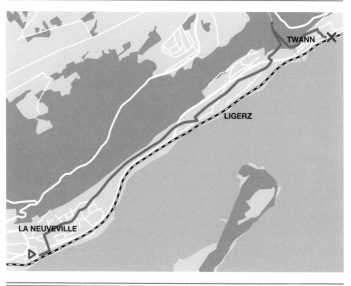

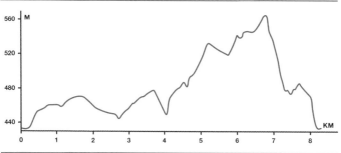

# DESCRIPTION OF THE ROUTE

 At the train station, with the lake behind, turn right onto Place de la Gare and follow it to the point where the street turns left. Continue past the cemetery, then a vineyard and turn right onto Chemin des Prés-Guëtins. Stay on this street, which climbs slowly; towards the end of the housing district, shortly before the vineyards begin, the street changes names to Route du Vignoble. This is a long ramble through the vineyards above the lake. A parallel hiking trail about 100–150 meters higher goes through the woods most of the time; the trail to follow is in the open with fine views and breezes off the lake.

The road takes a dip down near the lake, then immediately heads back uphill right after a group of houses at Chavannes Schafis. Continue through the vineyards along Chemin des Pèlerins, across a small river (the French/German language line) and the cog railway line; continue on what is now called Pilgerweg. At the church, just after the path joins Charrière, take the lower road, Rossweg, which soon becomes a footpath. Stay left on Rossweg when the path splits and keep climbing gently. The path joins a small road, Neuweg. Continue until the road is joined on the right by Schernelzstrasse – stay on this road when Neuweg goes off to the right. The road bends left around a vineyard. Take a right onto Riedweg here, away from the houses. The trail goes through fields and vineyards to the woods, where the footpath takes a sharp left at the edge of the woods – follow trail signs for Twannbachschlucht. The trail arrives at a point where this lovely gorge has a series of small waterfalls cut into the rock.

Cross the water following trail signs, heading for Twann – the other signed trails go higher and away from the village. (An alternative, but it adds about four kilometers, is to follow signs to the Gorges de Douanne, a lovely waterfall.) The trail heads back down the other side of the Twannbach river parallel to the path just taken, to Neuweg. This feeds into the two-lane Rebweg: turn left here and walk with woods on the left, vines on the right, until a smaller road called Rebenweg splits off to the right and heads downhill towards Twann. When a footpath appears to the right, take it: it leads straight down into the village. Turn left at Dorfgasse. The winery is on the left.

**Return**
It's a five-minute walk to the combined station for rail, bus and boat service.

**Notes**
This is the perfect hike for those who are looking essentially for a pleasant day out. The walk is comfortable, the views wonderful, the winery at the end very special.

# SCHOTT WEINE

Anne-Claire Schott's father made a name for himself in the region for traditional quality wines from vineyards on very steep slopes that are difficult to work. His daughter took over in 2016 and has quickly become something of a celebrity in the Swiss wine world. The winery is small, at 4.5 hectares of grapes worked, everything is done by hand, and natural wines are very much the approach. The winery is biodynamic, certified by Demeter. As more wineries experiment with this approach to wine, they look for successful pioneers in Switzerland and the Schott winery is held up as an example. Her line of *Aroma der Landschaft* is not so much experimental as the result of a dogged determination to focus on the best that grapes can give us with the least intervention – but don't read that as less work, rather as more! Schott brings to her work the sensibilities of an artist and an appreciation for wine as part of culture, thanks to her pre-vigneron training, having studied art and sociology. Philosophy and beauty have strong roles here.

 **Aroma der Landschaft Sauvignon-orange:** Let tasting here serve as a fine introduction to orange wines, and to natural wines, for those who are not yet familiar with them. The colour has an orange tint from leaving grape skins and seeds in contact with the juice during fermentation, thus the orange label. But the emphasis here is creating wines that speak of the terroir using a "natural" process: organic growing, handpicked, no added sulphites, natural (wild) yeasts.

## ADDRESS

**Anne-Claire Schott**
Dorfgasse 47
2513 Twann
Tel: 032 315 5217
info@schottweine.ch
schottweine.ch

## WINERY FEES

No. Regular hours and by appointment.

## WHERE ELSE TO FIND THIS CELLAR'S WINES NEARBY

**Sauvage**, Zentralstrasse 19, 2502 Biel,
032 510 10 66
info@sauvage-biel.ch

# WEST GERMAN-SPEAKING

# MUTTENZ

## UP AND DOWN, AROUND BASEL'S BUCOLIC COUNTRYSIDE

Zinggibrunngraben

BASEL

| ▷··· STARTING POINT | ···✕ DESTINATION |
|---|---|
| **LIESTAL TRAIN STATION** | **WEINGUT JAUSLIN CELLAR, MUTTENZ** |
| 📅 SEASON | 🎫 HIKE TYPE |
| **YEAR-ROUND** IF NO SNOW, BUT BEST **APRIL TO NOVEMBER** | **MODERATE** 🥾 |
| ⛰ MAP REFERENCE | ⏱ DURATION |
| **SHEET 213T** | **3H** |
| | ↦ LENGTH |
| | **10.6 KM** (PLUS 1.4 KM TO REACH THE IN-TOWN SHOP) |
| 🔍 INTERESTING SIGHTS | ∿ CLIMB / DESCENT |
| TRADITIONAL FARM ARCHITECTURE. ORGANIC ORCHARDS, FIELDS AND VINEYARDS. CASTLE RUINS. | **387 M / 392 M** |

## HOHLE GASSE
## PINOT NOIR
### WEINGUT JAUSLIN

RED

INTENSE WITH STONE
FRUITS (PLUMS),
SLIGHT TOAST NOTES

EXEMPLARY FRUITINESS WITH STONE
FRUITS, RED FRUITS, SOMETIMES
KIRSCH AND CHOCOLATE, SMOOTH
TANNINS AND A HINT OF SOURNESS,
VERY ELEGANT FINISH

DRY,
STILL

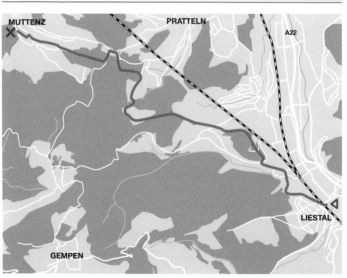

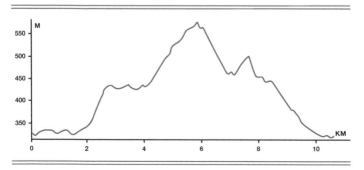

# DESCRIPTION OF THE ROUTE

From the train station, cross the tracks and head right through a residential area. Follow signs for the Tierpark and Baselland Psychiatric hospital, taking the footpath that leads to both. Walk through the Tierpark's charming small collection of animals. Head uphill on the footpath to the left, then turn right, downhill and along Bienentalstrasse.

Continue straight to a T-junction, where the trail heads left. It moves through a small housing development. Turn right at the Bienenberg road and uphill towards the small woods, Bienenbergwald. Continue along this road, crossing over Schauenburgerstrasse. The road becomes a trail through the woods. Keep a careful eye on signposts, as there are many hiking trails in this area and end-points often have similar names. Aim for the castle ruins of Neu Schauenburg and the hamlet of Schauenburg.

Once past the beautiful, large old farm, the road wraps around as it goes downhill. Avoid the footpath to the left and through the woods marked Hornweg. Instead, take a right turn to follow signs for Eglisgraben. This is suddenly horse country; single riders as well as horses with buggies share the trail. When you come out of the forest to a road, Schauenburgerstrasse again, turn left and stay on the road, past the Egglisgraben stables and restaurant. Shortly after, at the T-junction, turn left onto Zinggibrunnstrasse. At the next T-junction, turn right to stay on Zinggibrunnstrasse. Beware that two parallel roads carry this name!

At Rietmattstrasse, at the Paradisum events center turn right and shortly after at Lättenstrasse take the first left, onto Langjurtenstrasse. Here you suddenly have a fine view of the vineyards that cover the south-facing slope of the Wartenberg hill. Continue on this small road until just after the first road to the right which leads up into the vines. Turn left at Gwidemstrasse, a small road that leads up to the intersection with Wolfenseestrasse and the winery.

**Return**

From the winery, it's a 1.4 km, 15-minute mostly flat walk to the family's tasting room in Muttenz. Public transport is available only as you reach the in-town winery, but from there, bus and train connections into the city of Basel are good.

# WEINGUT JAUSLIN

The winery, a bustling family operation, is a regular supplier to the Basel area gastronomic restaurant business. The hike ends at the cellar, which is quite close to the beautiful vine-covered and south-facing Wartenberg hillside, shared by several grape-growing families. This working cellar is not always an easy place for tasting the wines, but the family has a good shop in the town of Muttenz itself, 1.4 km away. Urs Jauslin's top of the line Hohle Gasse Pinot Noir Grand Cru is made from selected clones and vines that are particularly well-placed in terms of soil and sunlight. The Burgundian influence is apparent, and the wines are excellent quality for what he points out is a far lower price.

 **Hohle Gasse Pinot Noir:** This wine was selected for the Mémoire des Vins Suisses, an honour given to wines capable of evolving well over time. It is a regular award-winner at competitions, including being named best at the Mondial des Pinots only 10 years after it was created: it is an excellent example of how suited Switzerland is to this grape. The style is similar to the Pinots of Burgundy, but Urs Jauslin has adapted it to ensure that it remains concentrated, retaining both fruit and freshness.

## ADDRESS

**Weingut Jauslin**
Baselstrasse 32 (the cellar is at Wolfenseestrasse 14)
4132 Muttenz
Tel: 061 461 84 35
info@weingutjauslin.ch
weingutjauslin.ch

## WINERY FEES

No

## WHERE ELSE TO FIND THIS CELLAR'S WINES NEARBY

**Restaurant Egglisgraben**, Egglisgraben 12B, 4133 Pratteln,
061 823 18 18
restaurant@egglisgraben.ch

# RIEHEN

## WILD URBAN FOREST TO DEEP CULTURE

BASEL

| | |
|---|---|
| ▷⋯ STARTING POINT | ⋯✕ DESTINATION |
| **BASEL SCHIFFLÄNDE** | **WEINGUT RIEHEN, RIEHEN** |
|  SEASON | HIKE TYPE |
| **APRIL-NOVEMBER** | **MODERATE /DIFFICULT**   |
| MAP REFERENCE | ○ DURATION |
| **SHEET 213T** | **2H 45M** |
| | ↦ LENGTH |
| | **10.4 KM** |
| 🔍 INTERESTING SIGHTS | ⌇ CLIMB / DESCENT |
| BASEL RIVERFRONT. HORNGRABEN RESERVE. WINERY ARCHITECTURE. | **221 M / 192 M** |

## CHARDONNAY
# LE GRAND
### WEINGUT RIEHEN

 WHITE

 VERY AROMATIC WITH NOTES OF PEAR, GRAPE, APPLE, HONEY, FRESH HAY

 FULL-BODIED WITH THE BIGNESS OF A GRAND CRU WINE, STEELY AND ACIDIC, LONG AND ELEGANT

 DRY, STILL

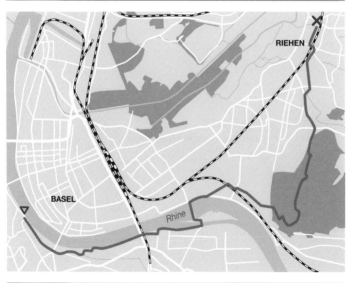

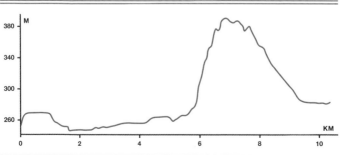

# DESCRIPTION OF THE ROUTE

The old town where the small ferries cross the Rhine, near the grand old hotel Les Trois Rois, is a good starting point; the trail goes through the old city, but there is a riverfront walkway on the opposite bank, so hikers can choose and cross back and forth for the first couple of kilometres. Start next to the Mittlere Brücke bridge and walk along Rheinsprung, Augustinergasse, in front of Münsterplatz and the gothic cathedral for which it is named. Continue along Rittergasse to the Kunstmuseum at St. Alban-Graben.

From the Kunstmuseum, continue straight then turn left onto Mühlenberg, right at St. Alban-Kirchrain, right briefly at the St. Alban church, left and over the canal to follow a slight zig-zag towards the river and the St. Alban-Rheinweg. Shortly after a small canal, continue to follow the footpath (water level of the Rhine permitting) rather than the street a riverside walk to and under the Schwarzwaldbrücke.

After the bridge follow the road, going left when it splits, onto Birskopf-weglein, and then take the road left onto Birskopfsteg. Follow it across the little Birs river to Birsköpfli. Turn left to follow the Marie-Lotz Prom-enade along the waterfront until Hofstrasse and the little bridge that leads across to Kraftwerk (power plant) island. Cross from the island to the right bank of the Rhine and continue to walk upstream to where the path joins Grenzacherstrasse, continue until Bettingerweg; turn left. At the end of the street turn right. At Hörnliallee turn left and immediately turn right after the train tracks to walk along the border just inside Swit-zerland. Friedhof Hörnli, the city's main cemetery and one of Switzer-land's largest, is on the left. Follow signs for Hornfelsen and Riehen Dorf. The trail takes you briefly into Germany then steeply uphill along the Buchsweg through the forest to a delightful spot with lounge chairs and benches where an open view over the Rhine and the city can be admired. Continue along the Buchsweg, following signs for Wenken-park and Riehen. Riehen municipality manages the well-groomed trails, but not the forest. Try to spot some of the 100-plus beech trees that are more than 100 years old and, suggests Pro Natura, "wild high-ways" through the shrub and climbing ivy that lead to the homes of badgers and foxes deep in the forest.

The forest path leads abruptly into the suburbs of Basel. When Ausser-bergweg leads out of the woods to a T-junction turn right and then take the left fork onto Bettingerstrasse. Follow it through Wenkenhof until Martinsrain. Turn right and at Wenkenstrasse, turn left. Continue until the railroad tracks at Eisenbahnweg; turn right and in a few metres take the fork to the right, then go left up to Schmiedgasse and turn left. After passing the Bahnhofstrasse intersection on the left, take Wendelins-gasse to the right and continue straight as it joins Rössligasse. The winery is a couple of blocks further on the left.

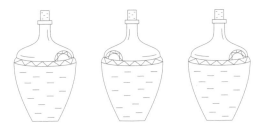

**Return**
Cross Sarasin Park next to the winery to reach the frequent trams with stops in front of the Beyeler Foundation.

**Notes**
The trail crosses into Germany and the Buchwald, through a nature reserve that joins the Swiss one. Beware that Swiss trail signs disappear during this part of the hike, replaced by less obvious German ones.

Children are likely to see the wildness of the Basel forest reserve as a playground, but areas off trail can be dangerous, so keep to the trail to be safe, but also for the sake of the wildlife for whom this is a real haven.

# WEINGUT RIEHEN

The winery has been remarkably successful in a short time. The town of Riehen decided to revive its winery and invited bids to oversee it in 2018. Winners Hanspeter and Edeltraud Ziereisen won the bid for wine production – they own a winery just north of Basel, over the border in Efringen-Kirchen, Germany – and Urs and Jacqueline Ulrich for administration. By 2020 the *Gault&Millau* guide had named this one of the 125 best Swiss wineries. Silas Weiss joined the group as a new part-owner and is responsible for the vineyards and the cellar. This is a small, intense operation; be sure to phone in advance for a tasting session. The vineyard is mainly behind the Beyeler Foundation, clearly visible from its large glass windows.

**Chardonnay Le Grand:** matured 10 months in barrels.

## ADDRESS

**Weingut Riehen**
Rössligasse 63
4125 Riehen
Tel: 061 303 0453
urs.ullrich@weingutriehen.ch
silas.weiss@weingutriehen.ch
weingutriehen.ch

## WINERY FEES

No

## WHERE ELSE TO FIND THIS CELLAR'S WINES NEARBY

**Restaurant Sängerstübli**, Oberdorfstrasse 2, 4125 Riehen,
061 641 11 39
info@saengerstuebli.ch

# ERLINSBACH

## "GIVE IT TIME" (2-PART HIKE: PART 1)

AARGAU

| ▷⋯ STARTING POINT | ⋯✕ DESTINATION |
|---|---|
| **WITTNAU, MITTELDORF BUS STOP** | **SALHÖHE, HOTEL IN ERLINSBACH** |

 SEASON

**APRIL-NOVEMBER**

 MAP REFERENCE

**SHEET 224T**

 INTERESTING SIGHTS

AARGAU JURA PARK.
VIEWS OF SWISS ALPS AND GERMANY.

 HIKE TYPE

**MODERATE**

🕐 DURATION

**2H 45M**

↦ LENGTH

**8.6 KM**

〰 CLIMB / DESCENT

**590 M / 214 M**

## THALHEIM CHALOFE
### TOM LITWAN WINES

 RED

 REDCURRANTS AND LEATHER, AN INCREASINGLY COMPLEX NOSE WITH AGE, WITH SOME BLUEBERRY, EARTHY NOTES.

 FRUIT MORE DISTINCTIVE, CONCENTRATED, ELEGANT FINE TANNINS, SMOOTH, AND THE BURGUNDY STYLE BECOMES APPARENT.

 DRY, STILL, OAKED 8 MONTHS

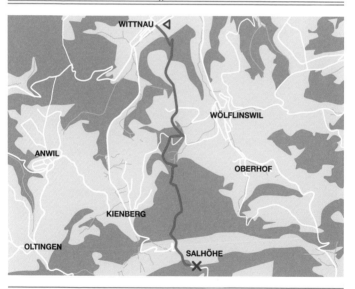

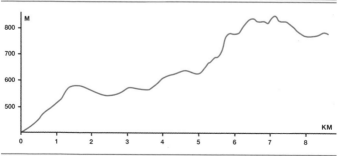

# DESCRIPTION OF THE ROUTE

With the village of Wittnau at your back, head up the hill, following the Regional Trail 42 signs, past farms and towards the woods on Gisletenweg. The trail starts off on a small paved road, but becomes a dirt forest road where the trees start. This area is crisscrossed with hiking trails and as a result with many yellow arrows, but number 42 is a long regional trail (this is section 6) and it's generally well marked. Salhöhe is the highest point, along a ridge, with a road, restaurant and bus service at the top, so when in doubt this is the sign to follow.

The dirt trail climbs and does a loop back to the left close to a small road before it briefly joins it, then loops back to the right and off the road. Continue climbing to a small road where the woods end and the clearing called Alteberg begins (do not take the trail to the left immediately before this point). Follow this mainly gravel and dirt path across the Altenberg plain – wide open space with cows and fields of crops. Cross a first road and continue on the trail as it skirts the edge of a pine forest, then at a second road take a sharp right, following the footpath into the woods; cross the same winding road soon after. Continue straight, ignore the

one trail option to the right – then at one point there is a clearing before the trail heads back into the woods. It gradually bends left and then takes a sharp right. From here, the trail zig-zags as it climbs about 100 meters in altitude to the Burgflue, a forest clearing above one of the high cliff faces for which the Jura Park is known, home to rare rock flora.

The trail continues through forest and clearings, mostly straight and climbing steadily, until it crosses the occasionally busy road to Salhöhe, just above a collection of farmhouses and barns. The trail continues, parallel to the road, until Salhöhe, a crossroads with a restaurant and large parking lot, a clue that this is a busy hiking area in summer.

### Return
From Salhöhe take the bus to Erlinsbach SO (Solothurn). The restaurant and bar, where Litwan wines can be tasted, sits right on the Solothurn/Aargau cantonal line.

### Notes
This is the first part of Regional Trail 42's section six, from Wittnau to Aarau. It is a fine trail through undulating countryside that shifts from fields to forests, climbing up and down the folded Jura hills. Note that part 2 starts at Salhöhe, where this trail leaves off; take the bus there and hike down for the second day, which also ends at Landhotel Hirschen. In total, this is close to 20 km and can, of course, be done in one day, in which case the stop at the Wehrli winery should be followed by the comfortable walk to Erlinsbach for a second tasting at the Hirschen. Note that Tom Litwan works with such a small team and the demand for his wine is so great that he can rarely meet clients, so he encourages people to taste his wines at what is popularly known as the wine hotel in Erlinsbach, where several of the rooms are sponsored and decorated by wineries. Both Litwan and Wehrli wineries have rooms here. Litwan himself will most likely be in the vineyards!

# TOM LITWAN WINES

Tom Litwan is the kind of "authentic" entrepreneurial artisanal winemaker that the wine world loves to discover and keep rediscovering: he makes superb wines, operates on a very small basis, sells whatever he makes to a handful of shops and restaurants, and doesn't have a place or time to welcome visitors. It doesn't hurt that he's a really nice guy who trained as a mason and who doesn't come from a winemaking family. "My family? They're more wine consumers," he chuckles. He took a handyman job at a small chateau in Chablis in Burgundy when he finished his masonry training, where he "discovered another world" and learned about everyday great wines. He then worked at a Geneva winery that was an early convert to biodynamic farming, and in 2006 he set up shop for himself in his native Aargau. By 2010 he was obtaining biodynamic certification and immersing himself in understanding vine parcel Pinot Noir and Chardonnay. His wines are not always easily accessible

when they are young, with wild yeasts from the winery that can give a yeasty smell, and some reduction, which can give a dubious smell when first opened. But these are wines that are designed for the long haul and when allowed to breathe and more importantly, to age, they are some of the most beautiful wines made in Switzerland. "Give it time, give it time," he says of the whole process, from vineyard to cellar.

# THE WINERY

This is a very small operation, with 5.5 hectares worked by the owner with the help of a couple who share a full-time position. In a normal year he makes 6 reds, 3 whites and 2 sparkling wines, about 15,000 bottles. The switch from masonry to winemaking came about when he realized that not only did he like working outside but that there was a challenge in seeing wine as an agricultural product that is part of what nourishes us, and that his job would be to accompany the product from vine to glass. His approach is on the surface uncomplicated – reds and whites are made in stainless steel with wild yeast, spend one day on their lees to settle and then 12 months in older Burgundy oak barrels. His Riesling-Sylvaner is exceptional: he seeks a dry and mineral wine that doesn't have the perfumes of more commercial versions. Same with his famous reds. "Give it time."

His business model is very straightforward: he works in the vines and cellar, outsources sales to a handful of excellent wine shops including one in Hong Kong. He doesn't have a space to receive visitors, nor is he set up to sell; instead, he works closely with the Hirschen wine hotel and restaurant in Erlinsbach for anyone who wants to taste his wines when in the area. Owner Albi von Felten is close to the winemaker, knowledge-able (ask about the winemaking process), and can offer some of Litwan's older vintages – a wine-tasting experience not to be missed.

 **Thalheim Chalofe:** Thalheim is the name of the village where the grapes are from and Chalofe the name of the vine parcel. The limestone with clay soil here is key to this wine, which reflects its terroir. There may once have been lime kilns on this spot; quicklime was used in the past to reduce the pH of soil and increase its fertility. The vigneron has nearly 20 years of experience with biodynamic growing and winemaking and has been Demeter-certified for several years. This, like his other wines, can in some years have a slightly stinky nose due to reduction, part of the wine-aging style he seeks, appreciated by some connaisseurs but not others. These tend to be the best vintages in the long run. Chalofe is best drunk when it is a few years old. At that point it develops the classiness one expects of a good Burgundy, which is where his winemaking path began.

## ADDRESS

**Hirschen Landhotel and wine bar**
Hauptstrasse 125
5015 Erlinsbach, Aarau
Tel: 062 857 3333
mailbox@hirschen-erlinsbach.ch
hirschen-erlinsbach.ch

## WINERY FEES

At the hotel wine bar and in the cafe, wine is available by the glass, the bottle, in a series: ask about the multiple options and expect to be impressed by the very long Swiss wine list.

## WHERE ELSE TO FIND THIS CELLAR'S WINES NEARBY

**Restaurant Landhotel Hirschen**, Hauptstrasse 125, 5015 Erlinsbach, 062 857 33 33
mailbox@hirschen-erlinsbach.ch

# KÜTTIGEN

## "DIVERSITY: MINERAL, FRUIT, IRON; LAKES, RIVERS, PLAINS" (2-PART HIKE: PART 2)

AARGAU

| ▷⋯ STARTING POINT | ⋯✕ DESTINATION |
|---|---|
| **SALHÖHE BUS STOP** (WHERE THE HIKING STOPS FOR PART ONE OF THIS TWO-PART TRAIL) | **WEINBAU WEHRLI, KÜTTIGEN** |
| 📅 SEASON | HIKE TYPE |
| **APRIL-NOVEMBER** | **MODERATE** 🥾 |
| 🗺 MAP REFERENCE | 🕐 DURATION |
| **SHEET 224T** | **3 HOURS** |
| | ↦ LENGTH |
| | **10.9 KM** |
| 🔍 INTERESTING SIGHTS | 〰 CLIMB / DESCENT |
| AARGAU JURA PARK. VIEWS OF SWISS ALPS AND GERMANY. | **282 M / 636 M** |

**RIESLING-SYLVANER**

# ESPRIT BARRIQUE AOC KÜTTIGEN
## WEINGUT WEHRLI WINES

WHITE

RIPE APRICOTS, PEAR, CARAMEL, VANILLA, ROASTING NOTES THEN CITRUS FRUITS

BEAUTIFUL ACIDITY, RICHLY MINERAL, SALTY AND A TASTE OF CITRUS FRUITS (GREEN LEMONS), UNCTUOUS WITH A LONG FINISH

DRY, STILL, FERMENTED IN BARRELS AND MATURED SEVERAL MONTHS IN OAK

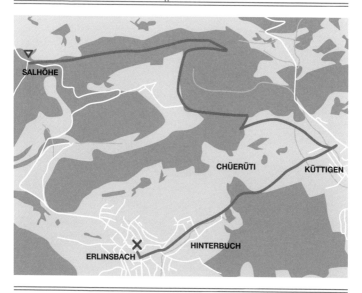

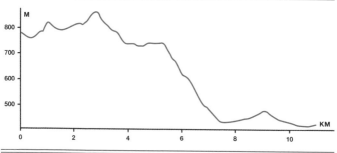

# DESCRIPTION OF THE ROUTE

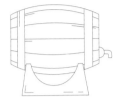

The bus stops at Salhöhe, a junction of roads with several hiking trails, a large parking lot and a restaurant. With the parking lot behind you, climb a few steps up to the ridge, from which Germany's Black Forest is visible on a clear day. Turn right, following arrows for Wasserflue and Küttigen, and go past an old cable car before continuing along the ridge trail, with woods to your right and fields falling away below. Follow the trail in a mostly straight line, across one small road but otherwise through the woods to Wasserflue, a mountain (843 m a.s.l. in the Jura range). The trail takes a sharp right here to avoid the cliff – later it's possible to look back at the cliff face, a good example of the geological feature of "mountain folds" that create the Jura hills in this area.

The trail descends gently but steadily from this point on, turning left then heading straight until a small road at Säägel, where there is a farm. The road goes straight for just a few metres; the trail turns left and carries on through a mix of woods, fields and rocky patches until it abruptly climbs down and the trail narrows to zigzag down a steep slope. It makes a final, longer sharp turn to the right. Soon after, the main trail – part of the regional hike 42 section from Wittnau to Aarau – continues straight, but this trail veers left to go to Küttigen. Simply stay

on the trail, which offers almost no options, to the edge of town. Ignore the first two roads to the right; at Brandackerstrasse turn left, cross the small Vorstadtstrasse and go a few meters: the winery is on the left.

To carry on to Erlinsbach after visiting the winery, turn right onto Brandackerstrasse and briefly retrace steps but stay on the road, a pleasant country road. At one point the main hike 42 trail crosses the road, which is now called Küttigerstrasse. Note the "Militär!" warning signs along the road, with a military shooting range about halfway to Erlinsbach. The road leads straight into the Oberdorf part of the town. At a roundabout take the third street to the right, Küttigerstrasse again, and go straight until Hauptstrasse. Turn right and just after the road bends left, Landhotel Hirschen is on the left.

### Return

There is bus service between Küttigen and Erlinsbach SO (Solothurn), so the last part of the hike can be cut short, after visiting the winery. Hirschen hotel in Erlinsbach, with its restaurant and winebar, sits right on the Solothurn/Aargau cantonal line. Wehrli wines can be tasted again here (or do it here rather than at the winery). The town has good bus service and it takes 25–40 minutes to reach the train station in nearby Aarau.

**Notes**

This is the second part of a trail that mostly follows Regional Trail 42's section six, from Wittnau to Aarau. It is a fine trail through undulating countryside that shifts from fields to forests, climbing up and down the folded Jura hills. Note that part one ends at Salhöhe then goes to Erlinsbach via bus. This trail begins at Salhöhe; take the bus there and hike down for the second day, which also ends at Landhotel Hirschen. In total, this is close to 20 km and can, of course, be done in one day, in which case the stop at the Wehrli winery should be followed by the comfortable walk to Erlinsbach to taste the Litwan wines at the Hirschen, where some older vintage wines from the Wehrlis are also available.

# WEINGUT WEHRLI WINES

Aargau has a curious winemaking history. In 1870 the government refused to allow more vines to be planted, arguing that the 450,000 litres produced were leading to drunkenness and that the land was needed for cereal crops. Phylloxera, the grapevine killer, followed, and the amount of wine made fell sharply. The Wehrli family, like others who want to bring back wine production, are very selective about where their grapes are grown. Their 11 hectares of vine are in three areas (Küttigen, Erlinsbach, Seengen) with very different soils; Aargau is remarkable for having nine types of soil and three climates. The Wehrli wines are clearly marked by these differences and are sold as terroir wines.

This is very much a bustling family business. Susi is an accomplished and much lauded winemaker who travelled widely and trained abroad, in addition to studies (Swiss federal maître vigneron). Her husband Franz Steiger went from a career in haute gastronomie to vigneron studies and he oversees the vineyard. Rolf, Susi's twin, is a trained mechanic who completed technical commercial studies, and his wife, with a hospitality degree and experience, handle administrative work. Susi and Rolf's parents remain active in the business.

**Esprit Barrique AOC Küttigen:** Riesling-Sylvaner is important to wineries in this region and, while in the past it could be too soft and a bit sweet, this is one of the very good newer versions. Aromatic but not sweet, mineral with excellent acidity. It's best drunk at 10–12C° to appreciate the balance.

## ADDRESS

**Wehrli Weinbau AG**
Oberdorfstrasse 8
5024 Küttigen
Tel: 062 827 2275
info@wehrli-weinbau.ch
wehrli-weinbau.ch

## WINERY FEES

Winery: no; regular hours.
At the Hirschen hotel wine bar and in the cafe, wine is available by the glass, the bottle, or in a series: ask about the multiple options and expect to be impressed by the Swiss wine list.

## WHERE ELSE TO FIND THIS CELLAR'S WINES NEARBY

**Restaurant Landhotel Hirschen**, Hauptstrasse 125, 5015 Erlinsbach, 062 857 33 33
mailbox@hirschen-erlinsbach.ch

# UNTERSIGGENTHAL

## GENTLE LIMMAT RAMBLE TO NEW-OLD ROMAN BATHS

AARGAU

| ▷⋯ STARTING POINT | ⋯✕ DESTINATION |
|---|---|
| **KIRCHDORF CENTER BUS STOP** | WEIN & GEMÜSE WEINGUT UMBRICHT, **UNTERSIGGENTHAL** |

| 📅 SEASON | HIKE TYPE |
|---|---|
| **YEAR-ROUND** | **MODERATE**  |

| 🗺 MAP REFERENCE | 🕐 DURATION |
|---|---|
| **SHEET 215T** | **3H 20M** |
| | ↦ LENGTH |
| 🔎 INTERESTING SIGHTS | **13.3 KM** |
| LIMMAT RIVERSIDE. HISTORIC OLD TOWN OF BADEN. BUILDING BY RENOWNED TICINO ARCHITECT MARIO BOTTA. | 〰 CLIMB / DESCENT |
| | **186 M / 197 M** |

**MALBEC BLEND**
PIRMIN UMBRICHT

RED

LIGHTER THAN MOST MALBECS, WITH SURPRISING NOTES OF BLACK CHERRY AND RASPBERRY

REFRESHINGLY LIGHT YET WITH GOOD STRUCTURE AND TANNINS; AS WITH THE WHITES FOR WHICH HE IS KNOWN, VERY CLEAN LINES, ALMOST TAUT

DRY,
STILL

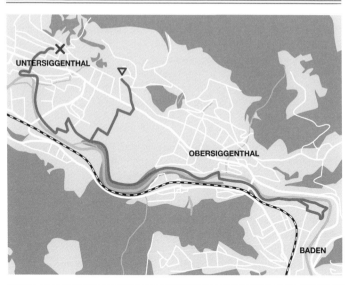

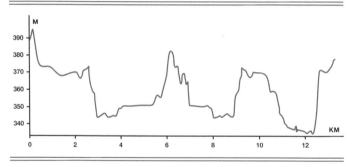

# DESCRIPTION OF THE ROUTE

Kirchdorf is a small, peaceful typical Aargau village whose large church marks the landscape; the trail starts next to it. Walk uphill along the Kirchweg and take the street on the right, Wiedackerstrasse, when the road splits. At the busy main road take a left and, immediately after, a right turn onto Studacherstrasse. Follow it as it bends around and take the small road that forks left, through open fields. At the T-junction turn right and then take the first left, which leads down to the river. Turn left onto the Wasserweg, follow the footpath down to the Limmat riverfront walk and continue until you come to the Kappelerhof Brücke. Although the footpath continues on both sides, it's important to cross here because there are no other easy pedestrian bridges until well past the center of Baden. Take the footbridge to the other side, over the lock and dam. Turn left and continue walking along the waterfront.

Shortly before the river takes a sharp bend to the right, and before the center of Baden, the trail offers two options, a path along the waterfront and a parallel path along the little bluff above. Take the lower path, which ends at the newly renovated Baden public baths. Just past the baths, turn right to explore the small old town, whose rich history seems outsized: the hot sulphur baths here have been famous since Roman times; scores of religious battles and European wars have seen settlements and treaties negotiated here, and for nearly 300 years, starting in the 15th century, the Swiss Diet, the cantonal representatives of the old Swiss confederacy, met in the town, making Baden something of a national capital. The town was invaded and razed and rebuilt time after time.

Leave the old town by heading back towards the river walk along Römerstrasse, turning right at Parkstrasse. Take the higher walking path along the river until it rejoins the waterfront via stairs (a sharp right for the staircase), then retrace the trail to the Kappelerhof Brücke, cross it and walk back along the riverfront. At Schiffmühlihalde, where the trail earlier joined the Limmat walk, carry on straight – the walkway veers away from the waterfront briefly, around a small industrial area.

Continue on the riverfront footpath until the river takes a large bend to the left, and soon after, the footpath ends at a T-junction: turn right to head uphill and into Untersiggenthal. At Höhenweg turn left then immediately right onto Kornfeldweg and continue to Schulstrasse then: first right, first left, first right, first left up to Dorfstrasse. Turn left and then right again to continue to the Umbricht family shop.

**Return**
Three bus lines share a stop a five-minute walk from the shop.

**Notes**
This is par excellence Swiss riverscape country: at Untersiggenthal the Limmat and the Reuss join the Aare, which is Switzerland's longest river

that rises and ends inside Switzerland. Soon after, the Aare joins the Rhine to flow towards Basel. With numerous gentle hillsides, woodland nature reserves and small waterfalls, it's a wonderful area to explore on foot. The hot sulphur baths in Baden combine nicely with hiking.

# WEIN & GEMÜSE, WEINGUT UMBRICHT

Pirmin Umbricht runs the family winery in Aargau; his brother runs the thriving family fresh vegetable shop and delivery business. The pair, in their mid-30s, are popular restaurant suppliers. Their father grew grapes and sold them; the winery/vegetable business is a project begun by the sons, who are keen to grow the firm with an emphasis on quality. Older brother Pirmin works mostly alone, with vineyards spread out around the region, offering him a mix of settings and soils for a varied wine lineup.

**Malbec blend:** Pirmin Umbricht is a natural experimenter, curious about what he can get his grapes to achieve, and this blend is one of his successes.

## ADDRESS

**The winery and shop Wein & Gemüse, Weingut Umbricht**
Dorfstrasse 55
5417 Untersiggenthal
Tel: 056 288 1479
info@wugu.ch
wugu.ch

## WINERY FEES

No

## WHERE ELSE TO FIND THIS CELLAR'S WINES NEARBY

**Restaurant Chämihütte**, Rooststrasse 15, 5417 Untersiggenthal, 056 298 10 35
hummel@chaemihuette.ch

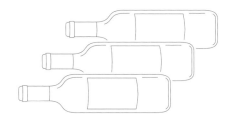

# EAST GERMAN-SPEAKING

# EGLISAU

## ELEGANT RHINE, TIMBER HOUSES, WOODS FOR WALKING

ZURICH

| ▷⋯ STARTING POINT | ⋯✗ DESTINATION |
|---|---|
| **EGLISAU TRAIN STATION** | **BECHTEL-WEINE, EGLISAU** |

|  SEASON | ⊞ HIKE TYPE |
|---|---|
| **YEAR-ROUND** IF NO SNOW, BEST **APRIL-NOVEMBER** | **MODERATE** |

 MAP REFERENCE

**SHEET 215T**

⊙ DURATION

**3H 15M**

↦ LENGTH

**11.4 KM**

🔍 INTERESTING SIGHTS

EGLISAU OLD TOWN.
TERRACED VINEYARDS OF EGLISAU.
BUCHBERG AND RÜDLINGEN – SWISS HERITAGE
SITES FOR THEIR HALF-TIMBERED HOUSES.
VIEW FROM RÜDLINGEN.

〜 CLIMB / DESCENT

**415 M / 430 M**

**BLAUBURGUNDER**
BECHTEL-WEINE

 RED

 RED FRUITS

 PLEASINGLY FRUITY
AND FRESH WITH
GOOD VOLUME

 DRY,
STILL

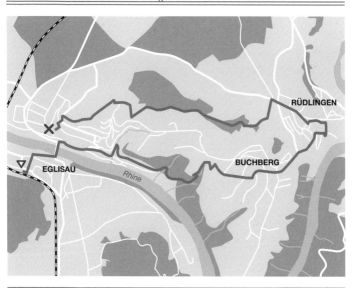

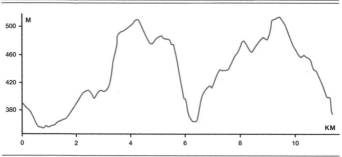

# DESCRIPTION OF THE ROUTE

Walk from the train station straight downhill on Bahnhof-strasse. The street bends to the right; at busy Zürcher-strasse turn left and cross Rheinbrücke, which offers a wonderful view of the Old Town of Eglisau. After the bridge take the first right turn onto Obergass and continue on this street through the old section until the road splits. Take the upper path, Weierbachstrasse, and immediately turn right onto Stadtbergstrasse. At the end of the vineyards the trail takes a sharp left and heads uphill on Langenbach-strasse, before making a hairpin bend to the right. Soon after, the footpath signs point to the left for the wine trail – instead, take the turnoff to the right onto Chlotenbuckstrasse and continue straight on a path parallel to the upper wine trail. The trail goes past several educational panels about the vineyards and Urs Pircher's winery, then ends after the winery, at Hinterer Stadtberg.

Turn left after the winery and head into the forest. Turn right: the woodlands trail begins here, initially with vineyards on the right and then, as the path becomes Hummelbergstrasse, the trail begins a relatively steep climb through the woods. It ends abruptly at a meadow and the footpath turns right, then right again. Veer away from the footpath by taking the first left turn, a farm road and then the first right onto Dorfstrasse, which heads into the small town of Buchberg. Follow the street for the length of the town. Where it bends to the left and Chilchenweg starts on the right, follow the footpath signs that lead down into Rüdlingen, with vineyards on the right. The trail follows this path along Bergstrasse; follow the yellow arrows as the path turns right and right again onto Schuelgässli. Take the first left and shortly after another left and continue along Hinterdorfstrasse to Oberdorfweg: turn left.

From here, the trail loops and begins to head uphill and slowly back to Eglisau. Turn right off Oberdorfweg onto Grabenstrasse. Continue to the hamlet of Steinenkreuz. Just to the right at the end of the street is an intersection: turn right and cross over Steinenkreuz, heading straight on Buchbergerstrasse. Immediately after the first street on the right is a footpath to the left. Follow this.

The footpath continues as a mostly flat walk virtually all the way back to Eglisau, initially across fields, then through light woodland, then along the edge of these small forests, first with the woods on the left and then, for some distance, with the woods on the right. The trail turns left and away from the woods at a place called Honegg. The footpath

becomes a small road. Just after Buckstrasse appears on the left, the trail turns right. The road here is named Honeggstrasse. At a Y-junction Honeggstrasse turns left; take the right-hand option. Soon after the road bears right; immediately after this, take a left turn onto Herren-holzstrasse and continue to the end of the road, turning right onto Galgenbuckstrasse. After walking alongside a vineyard on the left, the road, now heading downhill, makes a loop to the left. Cross Wilerstrasse and walk downhill, turning left onto Promenadenstrasse. Turn right onto the small path called Breitistäge. The winery is across the road on Rebbergstrasse.

**Return**
The winery is within meters of bus service.

**Notes**
For nature lovers, an area to explore near Rüdlingen, across the river, is Thurauen with its nature center (Flaach) and the confluence of the Rhine and Thur rivers.

# BECHTEL-WEINE

Mathias Bechtel is one of Switzerland's up and coming wine producers, named by *Gault&Millau* as a rookie of the year in 2018 and three years later labelled by them as one of the top 150 winemakers in the country. He moved to Eglisau in 2008 and worked for Urs Pircher, one of the country's best wine producers (the trail goes through his vineyards and past his winery), and they are now neighbors. Despite its relatively small size with 3.6 hectares, the Bechtel cellar produces 20 wines. Among them are Pinot Noirs in different styles and bottle sizes.

 **Blauburgunder:** This is the straightforward, good value for money little sister to the winery's classy Pinot Noir, a more voluminous well-structured wine. His Pinots are happily available in a variety of sizes, and this one comes in 50 cl, useful for those on the road. The south-facing steep slopes in Eglisau provide fully mature grapes that lend themselves to top-quality wines.

## ADDRESS

**The winery Bechtel-Weine**
Bechtel-Weine
Rebbergstrasse 18
8193 Eglisau
Tel: 043 810 7025
info@bechtel-weine.ch
bechtel-weine.ch

## WINERY FEES

No

## WHERE ELSE TO FIND THIS CELLAR'S WINES NEARBY

**Gasthof Hirschen**, Untergass 28, 8193 Eglisau,
043 411 11 22
gasthof@hirschen-eglisau.ch
**Hotel Restaurant Bahnhof**, Bahnhofstrasse 9, 8193 Eglisau,
044 867 01 05
andrehilber64@gmail.com
**Moema Gourmet**, Untergass 1, 8193 Eglisau,
044 829 21 60
info@moema.ch

# MEILEN

## A BOW TO THE SWISS HIKING TRAIL SYSTEM

ZURICH

| ▷⋯ STARTING POINT | ⋯✕ DESTINATION |
|---|---|
| **FORCH TRAIN STATION** | **SCHWARZENBACH WEINBAU, MEILEN** |

 SEASON

**YEAR-ROUND**
UNLESS SNOW

 HIKE TYPE

**MODERATE**

🕐 DURATION

**3H 45M**

 MAP REFERENCE

**SHEET 226T**

↦ LENGTH

**14.2 KM**

🔍 INTERESTING SIGHTS

PFANNENSTIEL.
JAKOB-ESS-WEG COMMEMORATIVE WALK.
JAKOB ESS MEMORIAL.
MEILEN LAKEFRONT.

〰 CLIMB / DESCENT

**346 M / 611 M**

# RÄUSCHLING SEEHALDEN
## SCHWARZENBACH WEINBAU

WHITE

FLORAL,
CITRUS FRUITS

FRUITY,
DISTINCTIVELY MINERAL,
WELL-STRUCTURED, TANGY
AND NOTABLY ACIDIC

DRY,
STILL

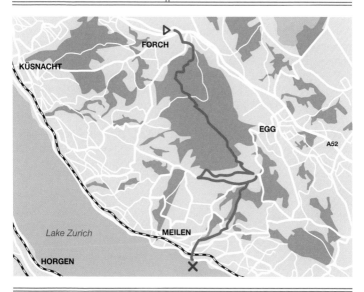

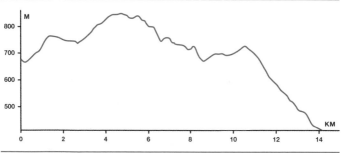

# DESCRIPTION OF THE ROUTE

Take the Forchbahn from the Stadelhofen station in Zurich. At the station in Forch follow yellow arrow signs for Pfannenstiel. Start on Kaltensteinstrasse and follow it into and through the small village of Kaltenstein. This is a very well-marked trail and for the most part, one must simply follow the yellow arrows up to the Pfannentstiel hilltop. Leave the village on Chisligstrasse; the trail briefly runs alongside Guldenenstrasse before heading to the right to enter the woods that lead to the top.

Place names and pathway names that the trail follows: Oberholz via Cholgruebweg; Cholgrueb is an area to the left; Stähli via Mittlere Stähli-weg. Turn right off Stähli-weg and the path soon takes a quick jog to the right, then to the left onto Chüelenmorgenweg. The path takes another right and then left over a small road (Guldenerstrasse). Continue along Wasenweg. Another quick right-left jog and the trail follows Schlagweg. The trail continues to climb gently in a mostly straight line at this point, with the path name changing to Stuckiweg, which leads to the high point of the trail shortly before Pfannenstiel.

Continue on Stuckiweg to the restaurant and picnic area at Hochwacht. Turn right to follow Jakob-Ess-Weg, a pleasant, well-marked commemorative trail (see Notes, below) mostly along the edge of the woods. Turn left onto Eichhaldenstrasse and at the next junction, take Herrenweg to the left, making a loop that returns to the restaurant area at Vorderer Pfannenstiel.

From here the trail leads downhill to Meilen. There are several ways down; retrace steps from the restaurant to the point where the road splits shortly after a bus stop, and take Schumbelstrasse to the left.

When the street takes a sharp bend to the left, follow the footpath that splits off from the road and start walking downhill. Shortly before Schumbel, re-join Schumbelstrasse and carry on along this road to In der Au, a small village; there is a *wanderweg* here that goes through the village to the right, but this trail skirts the village, so stay left and walk down Austrasse. When the road splits, take Stocklenweg to the right. Cross the larger road, Bergstrasse and continue straight along Seidengasse and follow signs for the railway underpass. Continue along Seidengasse to Seestrasse, where there is a bus stop: turn left here and the winery is on the left a few metres later.

**Return**
Bus stops are nearby. The train station is a 15-minute walk.

**Notes**
This has long been a classic hike for Zurich residents who want a day away from the city. It took on a special significance in 2018 when Forch to Meilen via Pfannenstiel was named a commemorative trail with one part named after Jakob Ess, the creator of the system of *Wanderweg* yellow arrows that are the hallmark of Swiss hiking trails. Ess was a teacher who took his students hiking and encouraged the Swiss population to stay healthy by walking outdoors. In 1932 he founded an

organization to promote a system that would mark national trails. Today the yellow arrows are part of a network that covers 65,000 km and, according to Suisse Rando, more than half of the Swiss population hikes regularly. The trail described here veers off from the classic one at the top, heading down through a residential and vineyard area to arrive at the winery on the southeast side of Meilen, close to Uetikon.

The trail can be shortened easily by 4 km simply by deleting the Jakob-Ess-Weg loop and heading straight to the Vorderer Pfannenstiel.

Alternatively, the commemorative trail continues from just above Toggwill, where the lake is suddenly spread out below to the Meilemer Tobel, a ravine with a large waterfall and a footpath that meanders alongside streams. It ends near the train station and from there a bus to the winery is an option.

# SCHWARZENBACH WEINBAU

This is one of Zurich's key wineries, well-known for its work bringing back Räuschling – long ago the canton's largest-selling wine until quality declined from over-production. Newer grapes replaced this older one and industrial zones appeared where vineyards had flourished. The winery also has an excellent reputation for Pinot Noir and Completer, but more than anything for being dynamic and innovative, with quality focused on terroir and selected grapes. They frequently work with other wineries to come up with creative new approaches to winemaking. The cellar also has a large line of distilled products, mainly fruit eaux-de vie but it includes an unusual marc from Completer and another from Räuschling.

The Schwarzenbachs have a remarkable collection of older wines. They were actively involved in developing the Mémoire des Vins Suisses in its early days; the original goal of this group of top Swiss wineries was to create a kind of bank to see how well their wines aged. An interesting claim to fame here is a yeast called 1895 that was discovered by Stikel Schwarzenbach. He and his wife, Cécile, recently handed the winery over to their son and daughter-in-law. The yeast was still alive when an 1895 wine was opened amongst professional friends – it has been carefully nurtured and is now sold to other wineries.

 **Räuschling Seehalden:** This can be a beautiful wine, perfect for lake fish; in the hands of the Schwarzenbach family, which has been refining this wine for five generations, the grape is shown at its best. They make a classic dry version, this more refined version, and a contemporary version where a bit of sweetness from the addition of some very mature grapes complements the sharp acidity. They also sell Räuschling R3, made by three wineries including the Schwarzenbachs'.

## ADDRESS

**Schwarzenbach Weinbau**
Seestrasse 867
8706 Meilen
Tel: 044 923 0125
info@schwarzenbach-weinbau.ch
schwarzenbach-weinbau.ch

## WINERY FEES

None for tasting in the shop; for a flat fee of CHF350 groups of up to 10 can take a 90 minute cellar tour.
Open Saturdays and by appointment during the week.

## WHERE ELSE TO FIND THIS CELLAR'S WINES NEARBY

**Restaurant Löwen**, Seestrasse 595, 8706 Meilen,
043 844 10 50
**Restaurant Alte Sonne**, Alte Landstrasse 57,
8706 Meilen,
043 539 57 28
info@altesonne.ch

# THAL

## WHERE THE HEARTLAND AND A STERN STONE RIDGE SHAKE HANDS

ST. GALLEN

| ▷··· STARTING POINT | ···✗ DESTINATION |
|---|---|
| **HEIDEN RACK RAILWAY STATION** | **ROMAN RUTISHAUSER WEINGUT AM STEINIG TISCH, THAL** |

| 🗓 SEASON | 🎲 HIKE TYPE |
|---|---|
| **YEAR-ROUND** | **MODERATE** |

| 🗺 MAP REFERENCE | 🕐 DURATION |
|---|---|
| **SHEET 217T** | **2H 15M** |

| | ↦ LENGTH |
|---|---|
| | **7.7 KM** |

| 🔎 INTERESTING SIGHTS | |
|---|---|
| RACK RAILWAY LINE (RORSCHACH TO HEIDEN). BIEDERMEIER PERIOD TOWN SQUARE. HEIDEN CHURCH. TYPICAL APPENZELL FARMS. STEINIGER TISCH | |

| | 〰 CLIMB / DESCENT |
|---|---|
| | **201 M / 572 M** |

# SAUVIGNON BLANC
ROMAN RUTISHAUSER
WEINGUT AM STEINIG
TISCH

WHITE

ELDERBERRY AND
GOOSEBERRY:
FRESH FRUITS

DELICIOUSLY TAUT, CRISP;
GRAPEFRUIT AND RIPE
EXOTIC FRUITS FINISH

DRY,
STILL

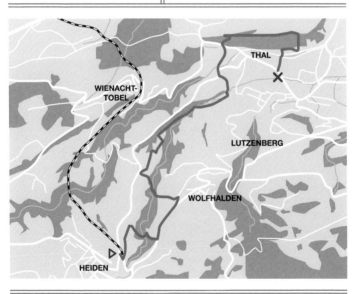

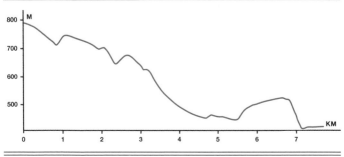

# DESCRIPTION OF THE ROUTE

From the Heiden railway station take Brunnhaldenstrasse to the left (the Bahnhofstrasse goes right) to the first corner and turn left onto Paradiesstrasse. Continue until it splits: take the right-hand fork (but not the footpath further to the right), which soon turns into a marked footpath. Head for Stöckli. From here down to Thal the trail skirts around villages and through fields and forest – immersion in the post-card-pretty Appenzell landscape! Shortly before Stöckli, turn away from the footpath and right onto the small road up through a forest to List. The trail goes along the edge of the little river Gstaldenbach, which momentarily widens here. Continue along the road, climbing through the forest with fields on the left, to a road, Wüschbach, and turn left. The road takes on the names of villages it passes: Kaltenbrunnen, then Luchten. The Luchten road splits off to the left and becomes a minor road: take it and continue to the corner of the Hinterdorf road: take a sharp left. The Vogelherd road, as it is now called, meanders down again through the Gstaldenbach woods, losing about 75 m of altitude. Continue to the small collection of buildings called Unteren. Turn right onto Gehrn and soon after, at the next collection of buildings, take the footpath to the left (if you miss this turnoff, don't worry – the Gehrn road becomes a footpath and meets up with this one).

Stay on the Gehrn road for some distance, as it winds around the hill-sides and eventually joins the Gstaldenbach River – it crosses the river after Hinterlochen and continues along the right bank, now in canton St. Gallen, on Bodenstrasse. Take a left to cross the river (there will be a farm building on the left) and follow the footpath, which goes more or less in a straight line, until a road: turn right here, onto Heidlerstrasse, then take the left (but not sharp left) footpath soon after, that leads across a small bridge, with several buildings on the right. Follow what

is now a small road, Käsiweg, across farmland, to Dorfstrasse: this is one end of the main street of Thal, and above it is the Steiniger Tisch, or stone table hillside, covered in vines.

Cross the road and follow the Krummbuechstig footpath up through the vines, to the top. Turn right and follow the signposted trail along the top, mostly light woods just above the rock wall. Continue to the Steiniger Tisch – take a minute to walk a little further to where you can see Lake Constance, Germany and Austria in the distance. Back at the restaurant, follow the signposted (Steinig Tisch Treppe) footpath, mostly steps, down through the vineyards, with the well-tended Rutishauser vines mostly on the right. At the bottom, turn right onto Weinbergweg, which turns left and goes alongside a pretty little farm and orchards to reach a small bridge. Cross it and continue straight on Hofäckerenstrasse to Dorfstrasse. The winery is just across the street.

## Return
A 5-minute walk to the bus.

## Notes
The winery is in a small town that is part of the semi-urban sprawl along Lake Constance, but it sits on the edge of the cantonal border with Appenzell, whose rolling hills rise right behind the winery. The trail connects these two, since from Steiniger Tisch the hills of Appenzell create a charming vista, and from these hills the unusual rock formation of Steiniger Tisch and its vineyards are clearly visible. This trail goes through open spaces and farm trails most of the time, making it a comfortable walk with dogs.

# ROMAN RUTISHAUSER WEINGUT AM STEINIG TISCH WINES

The family business was started by Roman's grandfather, a nursery man who added grapes to his great love of roses – he is responsible for having planted roses the length of the vineyard trail steps on the Steiniger Tisch; Roman's father Christophe, who is still active in the business, developed it as a professional winery. Roman, who took over in 2015 after an earlier career as a chef, was named Swiss Rookie of the Year in 2019 by *Gault&Millau*. From the beginning the family has made biodiversity and sustainable growing practices a feature; Roman's understanding of food and wine pairings has helped him develop excellent wines, including disease-resistant PIWI ones, which work well for restaurants. Between the roses and efforts to make the vines part of a larger landscape rich in plant and animal life, the Rutishauser vineyards are among the prettiest in the country, a bonus for hikers.

**Sauvignon Blanc:** The winemaker would argue that while this is a bestseller, it's not his best wine – of course not, as he makes very fine Pinot Noirs, among other things. But this is a good example of the quality of the work being done by this young winemaker.

## ADDRESS

**Roman Rutishauser Weingut am Steinig Tisch**
Dorfstrasse 17
9425 Thal SG
Tel: 071 888 1733
info@rutishauser-weingut.ch
rutishauser-weingut.ch

## WINERY FEES

No
Regular but limited hours or by appointment.

## WHERE ELSE TO FIND THIS CELLAR'S WINES NEARBY

**Ausflugsziel Steiniger Tisch**, Felsenstrasse 4, 9422 Staad / 9425 Thal, 071 888 12 05
info@stinigertisch.ch
**Restaurant Löwen**, Töberstrasse 1, 9425 Thal,
076 727 71 51

# MAIENFELD

## GO DEEP: GORGES AND ANCIENT SULPHUR HOT SPRINGS

GRAUBÜNDEN
BÜNDNER
HERRSCHAFT

| ▷··· STARTING POINT | ···✕ DESTINATION |
|---|---|
| **BAD RAGAZ,** START OF THE BADWEG THAT LEADS UP INTO THE TAMINA GORGE | **MÖHR-NIGGLI WEINGUT, MAIENFELD** |

| 📅 SEASON | HIKE TYPE |
|---|---|
| **APRIL TO NOVEMBER** | **DIFFICULT** |

| 🏔 MAP REFERENCE | 🕐 DURATION |
|---|---|
| **SHEET 237T** | **4H 30M** |

| 🔍 INTERESTING SIGHTS | ↦ LENGTH |
|---|---|
| | **15.5 KM** |

TAMINA GORGE. ALTES BAD PFÄFERS.
ST. EVORT CHAPEL. WARTENSTEIN CASTLE RUINS.
THERMAL BATH HOTELS.
WINE VILLAGE OF MAIENFELD.

| 〰 CLIMB / DESCENT |
|---|
| **591 M / 581 M** |

# PILGRIM
## MÖHR NIGGLI WEINGUT

RED

DEEP, RICH RED BERRIES
ON THE WILD SIDE

LUSCIOUSLY DEEP,
LONG,
SLIGHTLY SPICY

DRY,
STILL

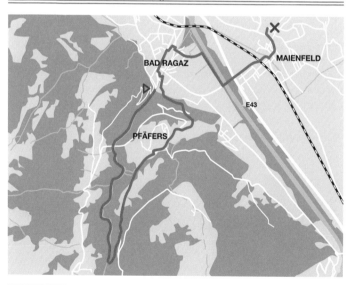

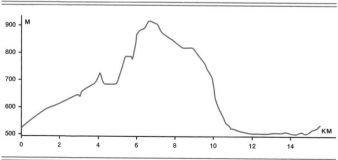

# DESCRIPTION OF THE ROUTE

The trail starts at the top end of the spa and art resort town of Bad Ragaz, where the Badweg walk through the Tamina Gorge begins. The first half of the trail moves gently uphill along an often shaded road for the occasional service vehicles and the postal bus, with woodland on either side, making it popular with dog walkers, families with strollers, and school groups. There are few alternative trails. The path narrows when the road ends at the Altes Bad Pfäfers restaurant and two museums, one to display the oldest existing Baroque thermal baths in Switzerland (no longer in service) and the other about the Benedictine Abbey which owned the baths for centuries.

At this point the path begins to climb more steeply; take the trail to the right and follow signs for Pfäfers via Naturbrücke. The bridge is simply a very short dirt walkway over the gorge. From here follow signs for Pfäfers – and prepare to climb up seemingly endless steps! The stairway suddenly tumbles onto a farm track road next to open meadow, an abrupt change of pace and scenery. Continue to follow signs for Pfäfers as the trail moves from the dirt track to the main road and into the town.

A few steps off the trail in Pfäfers is the 14th century Kapelle St. Evort, renowned for its artwork. Carry on towards the old hilltop Benedictine Abbey that overlooks Bad Ragaz, now part of the cantonal psychiatric hospital. Follow signs for Ruine Wartenstein at the bend in the road by the hospital – the Rhine valley is suddenly spread out below – and

continue towards the ruins of this castle that once kept an eye on the old Roman trade route and military trails.

The trail continues downhill through steep woods to rejoin Bad Ragaz, a town of delightful architecture that bears witness to its heyday as a 19th century resort. The town was created by the canton, which took over the old thermal baths from the Benedictine Abbey in the first half of the 19th century and in 1840 opened a 4 km road, the Badweg, to supply the town below with water piped from the hot springs. The public baths today are free for hotel guests; some hotels also have private ones. Walk through town, noting the artwork large and small along the Bahnhofstrasse. Opposite to Grossfeldstrasse, turn onto an alley called Kirchgasse on the right (not to be confused with an earlier Kirchgasse at the high end of Bahnhofstrasse), then take the first left onto – the other Kirchgasse! At Natschengässli turn right and then take the first right and then the first left onto Sandstrasse. Follow this street over the canal and continue straight on the other side; the street name changes to Seestrasse as you enter the park area that borders the Rhine. Continue to the waterfront and follow the footpath to the right, with the Rhine on the left and golf courses on the right. At the bridge, go up to the busy road and take it over to Maienfeld and canton Graubünden.

A small industrial zone is followed by the train station on the right. After the road takes a sharp bend to the right, at the intersection of Landstrasse and Aeuli, turn left to walk up through the old town. Schloss Maienfeld is on the left, as is Klostertorkel, as the street changes name, first to Stutz, then to Städtli, and to Steigstrasse. At the Fläscherstrasse intersection with the Lipp winery and distillery shop, the road bends right. Continue to the next corner where the winery is on the right.

### Return

The winery is a five-minute walk from the Maienfeld train station and regional buses.

### Notes

This is a straightforward walk up one side of the Tamina gorge and down the other along a bluff – medium difficulty except that the walk includes an impressive number of wooden stairs after the Naturbrücke. At Altes Bad Pfäfers, there is a worthwhile detour (450 m each direction) which takes visitors to the grottos (Taminaschlucht) where the hot springs come out.

Bad Ragaz is at the south end of Canton St. Gallen; Maienfeld is part of Graubünden, which can come as a surprise given that the city of St. Gallen is much further north, quite close to the German and Austrian borders.

# MÖHR NIGGLI WEINGUT

Matthias and Sina Gubler-Möhr are from longtime winemaking families and they make a collection of standout Pinot Noir wines, craftsmanship at its best. Their style is influenced in part by the long years they spent in California and the fact he grew up in Basel and some of their wines are made from Basel grapes. Conversations quickly turn to soil: geologically speaking, Basel is part of the northern Jura and the soil on the steep slopes where their famous Clos Marta grapes are grown is red. Matthias Gubler describes it as "old ocean soil", rich in iron, poor in limestone. Pilgrim is their top of the line Graubünden Pinot Noir, able to compete with the best in this region which is world-famous for its Pinots. The soil changes little from one village to another, but micro-climate differences can have an impact.

 **Pilgrim:** The vines in Maienfeld are relatively high, 550–600 metres and over 30 years old; grapes are handpicked with a large proportion left stemmed. Large vats are used for fermentation and the wine matures in barrels for 16–18 months. Pinot Noir grape, fermented in oak and barrel-matured for up to 18 months.

## ADDRESS

**Möhr-Niggli Weingut**
Steigstrasse 22a
CH-7304 Maienfeld
Tel: 081 330 1083
Mobile Sina: 079 705 9728
Mobile Mattias: 079 641 0132
Info@moehr-niggli.ch
moehr-niggli.ch

## WINERY FEES

No

## WHERE ELSE TO FIND THIS CELLAR'S WINES NEARBY

**Alter Torkel**, Jeninserstrasse 3, 7307 Jenins,
081 302 36 75
genuss@alter-torkel.ch
**Restaurant Falknis**, Bahnhofstrasse 10, 7304 Maienfeld,
081 302 18 18
info@restaurantfalknis.ch

# JENINS

## THE REAL (FICTIONAL) HEIDI, BÜNDNER HERRSCHAFT

GRAUBÜNDEN
BÜNDNER
HERRSCHAFT

| ▷··· STARTING POINT | ···✗ DESTINATION |
|---|---|
| **FLÄSCH BUS STOP** | **WEINGUT EICHHOLZ, JENINS** |
| 🗓 SEASON | 🎲 HIKE TYPE |
| **YEAR-ROUND** | **EASY** |
| ⌂ MAP REFERENCE | ⊘ DURATION |
| **SHEET 238T** | **2H 20M** |
| | ⊢ LENGTH |
| ⦿ INTERESTING SIGHTS | **8.5 KM** |
| BÜNDNER HERRSCHAFT. HEIDI'S HOUSE AND GOAT HUT. | ∿ CLIMB / DESCENT |
| | **291 M / 263 M** |

PINOT NOIR

# ALTE REBEN
## WEINGUT EICHHOLZ

RED

RED BERRIES,
BLACK CURRANTS
AND DELICATE HERBS

ELEGANT,
VERY CLASSY,
HARMONIOUS,
GOOD BALANCE

DRY,
STILL

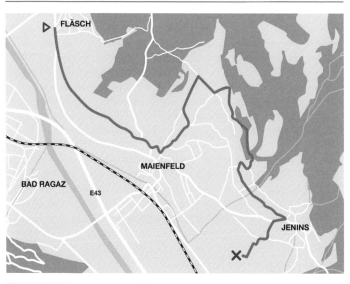

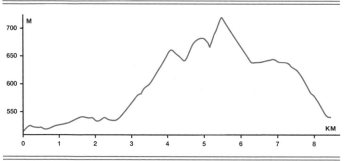

# DESCRIPTION OF THE ROUTE

From the bus stop in Fläsch – a village with so many very good wineries that it might be hard to set out on the road – follow signs for the main footpath and wine trail to Maienfeld. Cross the canal and step into a world of vineyards. The well-marked walking route is popular with locals, especially dog walkers, as it is mostly flat with fine views. Continue along the trail, which goes into the top end of Maienfeld, skirting the center at Vorstadtgasse, turn left.

Continue to the first Y-junction and take the right fork along Bovelgasse. Soon after there is a second Y-junction; stay on Bovelgasse and keep walking in what is now open country again until the next Y-junction: take the left fork. Continue straight to a T-junction and turn right. The road leads to Heidihof, which is heavily signposted throughout the area, a very popular tourist attraction. This is the re-creation of the farmhouse and goat shed similar to that in the book *Heidi* by Johanna Spyri. Walk past the statue and small park dedicated to Heidi and up to the Heidihof, and carry on up the narrow, steep footpath, following signs for Heidialp.

The alp itself, in open pasture land at the top of the hill some 450 meters higher, offers a lovely view. It is an idyllic spot in which to imagine the young girl Heidi in summer. The walk up, however, is not particularly interesting, as it follows a road that zigzags through woodland that changes little. The trail therefore turns off from the road at the first sharp left bend in order to follow a footpath marked for Jenins. Although it is possible to climb higher and take footpaths down to Jenins, they are rough and less well marked and sometimes involve crossing fields with cows, not a good idea in calving season.

The marked trail instead leads through a small patch of woods, coming out onto farmland with fields and small herds of cows and sheep, first along footpaths, then small roads. Cross a small stream and these bucolic scenes begin to give way to the vineyards of Jenins. Follow Ober-er-Rofelserweg into the central plaza in the town (the bus stop is here).

Turn right and continue downhill, past two restaurants on the right, to Alter Torkel restaurant on the left: turn left to walk through the vineyards. Halfway down, at the intersection of two of these small roads, turn right and then left. The large building of the winery is visible from the trail, so it's easy to visually find the way down.

**Return**
There is a bus stop in the center of Jenins, or walk on to Malans (35 minutes).

**Notes**
This is a good family hike and all but the section between Heidihof and the canal can be done with a stroller.

Good to know: a winery in this region is often referred as a "torkel".

# WEINGUT EICHHOLZ

Irene Grünenfelder, who early on earned the winemaking community's respect as a self-taught vigneronne who produced top-quality wines, has become something of a legend in German-speaking Switzerland for her small collection of handmade wines. She works with Johannes Hunger, her son, the "technical expert". This is a small winery and although they are open regularly on Saturday mornings, it is essential to make an appointment.

**Alte Reben:** matured 12 months in barrels. Another Pinot here is made from Burgundy clone grapes, but this one is from a Swiss selection (clones), making these two exceptionally good wines interesting to compare.

## ADDRESS

**Weingut Eichholz**
Eichholz 2,
7307 Jenins
Tel: 079 759 89 73
info@weinguteichholz.ch
eichholz-weine.ch

## WINERY FEES

No

## WHERE ELSE TO FIND THIS CELLAR'S WINES NEARBY

**Alter Torkel**, Jeninserstrasse 3, 7307 Jenins,
081 302 36 75
genuss@alter-torkel.ch

# MALANS

## STROLL SOFTLY: EARLY URBAN HISTORY AND MODERN FARMS

GRAUBÜNDEN
BÜNDNER
HERRSCHAFT

| ▷⋯ STARTING POINT | ⋯✗ DESTINATION |
|---|---|
| **CENTRAL SQUARE MALANS BUS STOP** | **WEINGUT DONATSCH, MALANS** |
| 🗓 SEASON | 🎲 HIKE TYPE |
| **YEAR-ROUND** | **EASY** 🚶 |
| ⛰ MAP REFERENCE | 🕐 DURATION |
| **SHEET 248T** | **2H 45M** |
| | ↦ LENGTH |
| 🔍 INTERESTING SIGHTS | **7.3 KM** |
| VINEYARDS. JENINS SMALL WINERIES. TOWN CENTER ART AND ARCHITECTURE IN MALANS. | 〰 CLIMB / DESCENT |
| | **170 M / 158 M** |

# MALANSERREBE COMPLETER
## WEINGUT DONATSCH

 WHITE

 CLASSIC – QUINCE, RIPE APPLES, ALMONDS

 DISTINCTLY ACIDIC WITH COMPLEX FRUITY NOTES AND SOME SWEETNESS

 MEDIUM-DRY, STILL

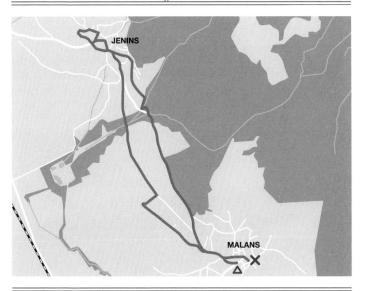

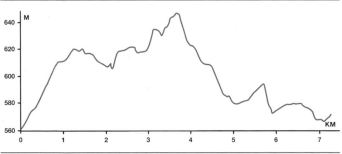

# DESCRIPTION OF THE ROUTE

From the bus stop, head west and away from the town square in Malans, which is a few metres uphill. Follow Kirchgasse until it becomes Jeninserstrasse (the right-hand, larger route option at the fork). Stay on Jeninserstrasse until it becomes Gassa, the right option at a fork. In front of the Älplibahn railway (cable car) station the name of the street changes again, to Jeninserstrasse. At this point take the hiking trail marked footpath and follow it all the way to Jenins. It runs parallel and close to the road, now again named Gassa, making this an easy trek for people with strollers; if the surface is a problem the road is a good solution.

The trail leaves the road at the second of two small rivers, the Selfirüfi; cross over and turn right to walk uphill a short distance, then left into the village. Jenins is a hilly old farm village and the trail goes up and down as it loops around this small but busy agricultural center. Follow several short streets: Pramalinis, Hinterwaldweg, right onto Alte Poststrasse, left onto Kreuzgasse, right at the main village corner onto the street called Ausserdorf which soon turns into Oberer Rofelserweg.

At the Jürg Obrecht winery turn around and retrace one's steps to the main intersection, turn left and head uphill turning left and quickly left again onto Plokweg and make a short loop either to the right or left. Head back again to the main intersection where the bus stops and from here head back to Malans. Walk downhill along Unterdorfstrasse.

At the next large intersection bear left and take an immediate right –
when the road splits right afterwards, go right along Malanserstrasse,
walking on the road (no sidewalk here) for a short distance. Two smaller
paved roads go off to the right: immediately after these, the trail leaves
the main road, going straight along a path that leads to Malans through
the vineyards. At one point the main path bends right and then left to
take a parallel but lower vineyard path: follow this. It becomes Oberer
Selviweg and leads into the center of town. From the town square, the
winery is about 100 meters along Sternengasse.

**Return**
Two-minute walk to the bus stop just below the town square, connections to the train station.

**Notes**
Donatsch, with its own 125-year-old wine tavern for food and drinks,
does not offer its wines at the new town square wine shop and tasting
bar. Call the Donatsch tavern ahead to reserve during busy seasons.

This is a beautiful walk on a fine-weather day, a stroll for anyone who doesn't want a difficult hike. It's a good walk for families with small children, including strollers, as most of the route is on paved vineyard or village paths and there is a playground and small park at the entrance to Jenins. Most of the wineries in Jenins are very small, albeit often with very good national and even international reputations, so the town walk offers a chance to get a better sense of how such fine wines come from such a small place.

# WEINGUT DONATSCH

Currently one of Switzerland's best-known wineries outside the country, thanks to its export business (few Swiss wineries are large enough to export) and reputation for top-quality wines: the Pinot Noirs have won several international prizes and are routinely given very high notes. The Chardonnays are equally admired. Martin Donatsch is also widely considered to make one of the best Completer wines, from a grape that nearly disappeared before a small group of growers saved it. The family has been making wine for five generations, with each contributing a new aspect to the work and building the reputation. Ask about the cellar, which winds around under the streets of Malans in a maze of connected cellars that belonged to several old houses.

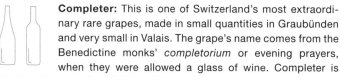 **Completer:** This is one of Switzerland's most extraordinary rare grapes, made in small quantities in Graubünden and very small in Valais. The grape's name comes from the Benedictine monks' *completorium* or evening prayers, when they were allowed a glass of wine. Completer is highly prized for its slightly oxidative nature and its ability to age remarkably well. This is a late harvest wine, but not made as a sweet dessert wine. It takes on honey notes as it ages, without added sweetness: a treasure and worth tasting if the opportunity presents itself.

## ADDRESS

**Weingut Donatsch**
Sternengasse 6
7208 Malans
Tel: 081 322 1117
info@donatsch-malans.ch
donatsch-malans.ch

## WINERY FEES

The winery's wine tavern, zum Ochsen, serves wine by the glass. For tastings: CHF18 for any four from the eight open wines offered. It also has a simple-but-good local fare wine and food tasting menu.

## WHERE ELSE TO FIND THIS CELLAR'S WINES NEARBY

**Chawi's Malanser-Stube**, Karlihofstrasse 2, 7208 Malans,
081 322 40 61
info@chawis-malanserstube.ch
**Restaurant Weiss Kreuz**, Dorfplatz 1, 7208 Malans,
081 735 25 00
info@weisskreuzmalans.ch

# MALANS

## SWITZERLAND'S "MOST VERTICAL METERS WITHOUT A STOP"

© FOTO NATUR-WELTEN SANDRA UND STEFAN KARP-GRÜNIG

GRAUBÜNDEN
BÜNDNER
HERRSCHAFT

 STARTING POINT

**ÄLPLIBAHN RAILWAY STATION IN MALANS**

 DESTINATION

**WEINGUT FROMM, MALANS**

 SEASON

**MAY TO OCTOBER OR NOVEMBER, ÄLPLIBAHN OPEN DATES**

HIKE TYPE

**DIFFICULT**

MAP REFERENCE

# SHEET 238T

DURATION

## 3H 20M

LENGTH

## 12.3 KM

 INTERESTING SIGHTS

**VIEWS OF GRAUBÜNDEN RHINE VALLEY.**

CLIMB / DESCENT

## 677 M / 1,869 M

# PINOT NOIR
# SPIELMANN
### WEINGUT GEORG FROMM

RED

BERRIES

BEAUTIFUL STRUCTURE,
LONG FINISH,
CASSIS AND BITTER
ALMONDS

DRY,
STILL

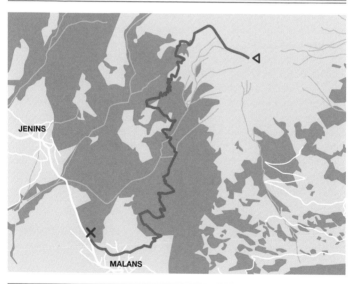

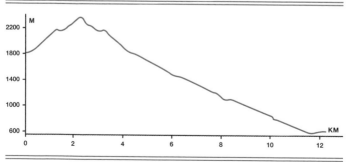

# DESCRIPTION OF THE ROUTE

Take the Älplibahn from its base station; the "train" is actually a small double cable car for only eight persons so be sure to reserve ahead. It covers the most vertical meters without a stop in Switzerland. It was originally a 3.5 km military transport system built in 1941. Its website notes: "In 1938 a road was built from the Austrian side up to the border; the Swiss border guards had to carry ammunition and food in an arduous ascent from Jenins to the mountain front." Money was quickly found to build, and forest specialists with experience working with ropes were relieved of other military duties to construct it. It has been renovated several times, with help from the Swiss Army. Today it is funded and run by volunteers.

The lower station is at 605 m a.s.l. in the Buochwald and the top station, where there is a restaurant, at 1,802 m a.s.l. The trail begins at the top and follows the standard easiest route, (marked red and white) to climb Mount Vilan, 2,375 m a.s.l. Allow at least two hours for the 3.5 km climb and another 1.5 hours to return the same way to the Älplibahn. Several popular high mountain routes start here. Expect to see serious hikers.

The descent to Malans: there is more than one option, but this trail takes the shortest route, which roughly follows the cable car. From the Älplibahn top station, follow signs for Malans. The hike stays close to the overhead railway as far as Älpliwald; head downhill through the Heuberg section, along the trail. The hike here is a mix of woodland and open stretches. (Where the trail splits at 1,245 m a.s.l., an alternative right-hand trail leads down to the Wynegg Castle ruins, which are just before a small river crossing, the Üll.) Continue along the trail, crossing one small river and ignoring three lesser trails, to reach the Älplibahn base station. The last 100 m of climb-down are through the top end of the village. Turn left onto Gassa just below the station, then immediately left onto Degenstrasse, follow it to the end and turn right onto Hintergasse. The winery is on the right after a few metres.

**Return**
The winery is a five-minute walk to the bus stop that is just below the town square with good connections to the train station in Landquart.

**Notes**
A good hike plus climb for those who want more than a pleasant stroll through the vineyards, although it can easily be combined with the Malans-Jenins loop to provide both. There is also a downhill hiking route from the top station to Jenins.

For mixed age groups, these two hikes can be a good solution: everyone takes the cable car up and those who don't want the alpine hike down can return via cable car and then do the gentler Malans-Jenins hike while the more sports-minded in the group climb Mount Vilan, then march down the mountainside. It's wise to make reservations for the cable car in mid-summer, Tel. 081 322 4764.

# WEINGUT GEORG FROMM

Georg Fromm was already a successful wine producer in Switzerland, running the family business, when he went to New Zealand to try his luck in Marlborough. He remained there for several years, continuing to oversee the Swiss family winery while becoming known as one of New Zealand's top producers of Pinot Noir. He returned to Malans with his New World wines experience and developed the Swiss business, which is now widely considered one of the country's best wineries, particularly for Pinot Noir (six of their eight reds are Pinots). They also run a guesthouse and his son Marco has joined him.

 **Pinot Noir Spielmann:** A perfect example of the kind of big, elegant Pinot Noirs that make this region famous.

## ADDRESS

**Weingut Fromm**
Oberdorfgasse 11
7208 Malans
Tel: 081 322 5351
malanser@weingut-fromm.ch
weingut-fromm.ch

## WINERY FEES

No

## WHERE ELSE TO FIND THIS CELLAR'S WINES NEARBY

**Sternen Malans**, the new village center wine-tasting café and shop, opened in 2022.

# KASTANIENBAUM

## GLASSWORKS TO ANCIENT REEDS

LUCERNE

| ▷⋯ STARTING POINT | ⋯✗ DESTINATION |
|---|---|
| **TRAIN STATION STANSSTAD** | **WEINBAU OTTIGER, KASTANIENBAUM** |

| 📅 SEASON | 🏃 HIKE TYPE |
|---|---|
| **YEAR-ROUND** | **EASY** 🚶 |

| 🗺 MAP REFERENCE | ⏱ DURATION |
|---|---|
| **SHEET 235T** | **2H 45M** (VARIES DEPENDING ON TRAIN CONNECTIONS) |
| | ↦ LENGTH |
| 🔎 INTERESTING SIGHTS | **9 KM** WALKING DISTANCE |
| GLASSWORKS MUSEUM, HERGISWIL. RIGI, BRUNNISTOCK AND PILATUS PEAKS. HORW PROTECTED ANCIENT REEDS LAKEFRONT AREA. | 〜 CLIMB / DESCENT |
| | **110 M / 96 M** |

RIESLING-
SYLVANER,
SAUVIGNON
BLANC

# LE PETIT
# MOUSSEUX
## WEINBAU OTTIGER

WHITE

PASSION FRUIT,
LIME,
ELDERBERRY FLOWER

LIGHT,
FINE BUBBLES

MEDIUM-DRY
SPARKLING

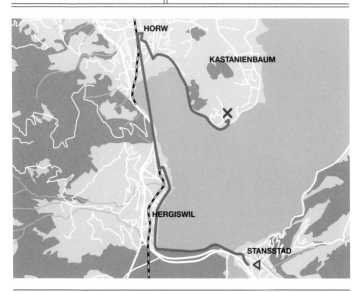

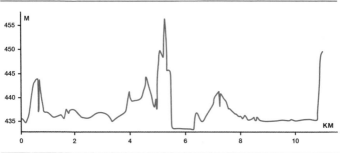

# DESCRIPTION OF THE ROUTE

From the Stansstad train station, turn left to head towards Hergiswil; follow the hiking path signs with the shortest hiking time, as this is the waterfront route. Walk parallel to the tracks along Bahnhofstrasse to Stanserstrasse and turn left. At the roundabout look for the walkway just after the second street: the street is a small and rather fun little loop around an exotic birds house, and the walkway next to it leads up to the road that crosses the bridge. Follow the cycling/hiking lane on the bridge; on the other side follow the walking path signs down to the waterfront. This is the start of Hergiswil's long Seestrasse. Follow it to the start of the town, where it bends right. Quite soon Glasi Hergiswil, the town's famous glassmaking business which began in 1817, appears. Walk down to the lakefront from the museum to enjoy the lakefront glass tower and a series of small water spouts. Allow some time for the museum, glassblowing demonstrations and shop.

Hergiswil is a busy little industrial center and the main street gives a good idea of the changes taking place with population growth and low unemployment. Walk past the center and look for signs to the Hergiswil Matt train station; turn left at or just after (two paths up) Mattli street and the station is a couple hundred meters away. Take the train from here to Horw, one stop, mostly through a tunnel.

In Horw, follow the *"Wanderweg"* sign at the station. With the tracks behind you cross over to Bahnhofstrasse and immediately take Bahn-hofweg on the right, then continue for several metres. Turn right onto Ebenaustrasse and follow it until a small canal. Cross this and turn left onto Promenadenweg, a very nice path that goes alongside the canal and that is popular with families and dog-walkers. Turn left at Seefeldweg, cross the canal and go across Rankried, turn left and immediately turn right. The street is called Winkelstrasse here but the name changes to Seestrasse when it reaches a hotel and the lakefront. Simply follow this lovely lakeshore walking path around the bend in the lake until a sign for the winery at Bergstrasse. Turn left and go up the steep but short road to the winery, which is on the left.

**Return**
10 minutes to the bus stop, service to Lucerne. One-hour walk to Lucerne city center.

**Notes**
This is a good family hike because there are interesting activities for children, small parks with playground equipment, benches and picnic tables – and the hike has a pause with a one-stop train ride in the middle. It's also very easy to follow the path without consulting maps too often.

It is possible to walk the entire route, but to avoid the rail and highway tunnel next to the lake at Matterboden, public hiking trails make a large loop around and above the tunnels, ending in an unpleasant industrial zone in Horw. Including the three-minute train ride from Hergiswil to Horw is by far the most pleasant way to do this walk around the lake.

The trail follows the main street, Seestrasse, through Hergiswil because the waterfront walks are not connected. There are several places where trail signs point down to the lake. These are all short loops to small parks or beaches, worth taking if you want a break from walking. Hergiswil is a regular boat stop for lake cruises; the dock is midway along the street.

# WEINBAU OTTIGER

Toni Ottiger opened the winery in 1981 and in January 2022 he sold it to two former apprentices turned employees: Kevin Studer and Denis Koch. The winery's name remains the same. Ottiger built up a business where the seven hectares provided four red varieties and four white, with several of the wines regular award-winners. One of the seven Pinot Noirs is in the Mémoire des Vins Suisses as a wine that ages well. Ottiger gained a reputation for being uncompromising on quality. He was an early convert to Solaris, a PIWI (disease-resistant) grape that caught on in the area, and today the winery helps some 25 small growers vinify their Solaris grapes; the region has become a center for the grape. The two new owners are determined to continue the tradition of high quality, while adding new wines that they believe will appeal to a new generation of wine-lovers – they're already en route, with very positive reviews and awards. The winery overlooks the lake with its vineyard surrounding it: a beautiful spot with views of the lake and peaks on three sides.

 **Le Petit Mousseux:** This is a relatively new wine in the lineup of nearly 30. It's a good reflection of the future here, with two former apprentices looking to create wines for new, younger drinkers. While the Pinot Noirs for which the cellar is famous remain firmly in place, they are being joined by natural wines, orange wines and this light-spirited sparkling wine.

## ADDRESS

**Weinbau Ottiger**
Breitenstrasse 6
6047 Kastanienbaum
Tel: 041 340 42 88
info@weinbauottiger.ch
weinbauottiger.ch

## WINERY FEES

No. Regular hours. Note that the wine is made 4 km away and to ensure someone is at the winery tasting room, it's wise to contact them ahead.

## WHERE ELSE TO FIND THIS CELLAR'S WINES NEARBY

**Seehotel Kastanienbaum**, St. Niklausenstrasse 105,
6047 Kastanienbaum,
041 340 03 40
hotel@seehotel-kastanienbaum.ch

# TICINO

# MONTE CARASSO

## WONDERS OF OLD MOUNTAIN VILLAGE LIFE RESTORED, TIBETAN BRIDGE

© BELLINZONA E VALLI TURISMO, LUDOVIC PIZZERA

SOPRACENERI

▷··· STARTING POINT

TOP OF THE MONTE CARASSO CABLE CAR, THE FUNIVIA: MORNERA STATION

···✕ DESTINATION

SETTEMAGGIO WINERY, MONTE CARASSO

📅 SEASON

**MAY-NOVEMBER**
FOR THE ENTIRE ROUTE

🗺 MAP REFERENCE

**SHEET 276T**

🔎 INTERESTING SIGHTS

TIBETAN BRIDGE.
CURZÚTT RESTORATION.
ST. BARNÀRD FRESCOES.
PUNCÈTÈ ARCHAEOLOGICAL SITE.
CHESTNUT FOREST PROJECT.

🏛 HIKE TYPE

**DIFFICULT**

⏱ DURATION

**3H 30M**

↦ LENGTH

**10 KM**

〜 CLIMB / DESCENT

**328 M / 1,420 M**

# TRIBUTO
## SETTEMAGGIO WINERY

RED

CLASSIC MERLOT DOMINATED BY FRESH BLACKCURRANT AND BLACKBERRY FRUITS, WITH NOTES OF COFFEE AND CHOCOLATE

FRUITY AND BEAUTIFULLY FRESH, BALANCED, SMOOTH TANNINS

DRY,
STILL

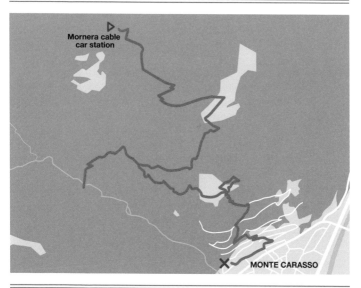

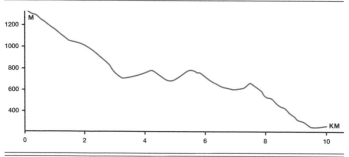

# DESCRIPTION OF THE ROUTE

The cable car leaves from Monte Carasso, which is next to Sementina. Mornera is the top stop; Pientina (1,000 m a.s.l.) and Curzútt (600 m a.s.l.) are intermediate stops. The descent from Monera to Curzútt is well-marked, mostly along open mountain trails with splendid views of distant Italian and Swiss Alps, hilly Bellinzona and the steep valleys to the north, as well as the towns below.

From just below the restaurant, turn left, following signs for the Curzútt footpath. The trail goes through the housing area, then turns right to zigzag down to a point just under the cable car, where it bends left; it continues to weave down, never far from the cable car, past buildings and through the forest. At the Pientina mid-station the trail sweeps left, then right through the woods and heads towards the collection of buildings and ruins known as Pcemuritt. Here it takes a sharp right, a left and a right again to walk through Pcemuritt. The trail heads back in the direction of the cable car, in large zigzags, following trail arrows – at one point it splits, and take the left option, which is longer but not as steep. The effects of drought and forest fire are visible on this part of the trail. Cross under the Funivia again, continuing down to Pcián de Rousg, just above the archaeological site at Puncète, which can be visited by taking a short detour either here or from the center of Curzútt.

Just after the ruins turn right where the trail offers three options, one of which is down to Puncète. The trail continues through the forest to Carasc, the Tibetan bridge, with some uphill hiking. There are two trails to the bridge from this side of the Sementina River; this is the upper one, and after visiting the site, the return trail takes the lower path. Simply follow signs to the bridge; the only alternative path, to the right, comes after the trail has gradually turned to the left – ignore the right-hand option. The return trip from the bridge retraces the trail for some time, until a well-marked option to the right for San Bernardo, the church, and the village of Curzútt. The church is 15 minutes from the village. Shortly after San Bernardo, stay to the left, where the trail splits, above the vineyard.

Once you reach the village the trail offers the option to walk around the village and slightly out into the forest before looping back: be sure to end up at the Funivia mid-station, which is where the marked trail down to Sementina begins. Stairs crisscross a path under the cable car; at Boccalign the Pairolo stop provides shuttle bus service April-October. From here, keep an eye on the cable car to ensure ending up in Monte Carasso next to the Funivia station, although the trail passes under the cable car five times. The trail is marked and cuts short several of the loops in the road by taking steps down between houses and on old tracks; either option works to reach the bottom.

From the cable car station head right along Pedmúnt for 10 minutes and the winery is on the right.

**Return**

The winery is just a few meters from the main road, with frequent bus service.

**Notes**

Don't be fooled by thinking this is "just" 10 km: this is a long climb down a mountainside, with rough footpaths and many, many steps for much of the trail. The downhill trek is very tough on knees; alternatives are to take the road from just after El Gasg (about halfway between Curzútt and Sementina) which has longer loops, or to take the cable car down from the Curzútt mid-station. The cable car doesn't stop unless someone inside pushes the button at the higher station, or if a person is standing on the platform, so be sure to go up the stairs to the platform! A shuttle bus operates, but infrequently off-season.

The Tibetan bridge is a hugely popular tourist attraction so this is a hike best done outside peak summer times – it can also be quite hot in this area in July and August. The bridge is well worth the hike, even if only to view it: 270 m long, 130 m high and beautifully constructed. It does move in the wind and from the movement of people crossing over it; it is not for those with vertigo.

The trail's main point of interest and worth the walk, even if the loop to the bridge is left out, is the old village of Curzútt, which had a population of 700 until the 1700s. Most life in the region was lived in the mountains, safely away from disease, power struggles and armies in Bellinzona, a major alpine pass town. Curzútt is a wonderful example

of the agricultural world that existed until 500 years ago, with beautiful (now restored) stone houses, small gardens, terraces for vineyards and grains, grazing land for animals, well-tended forests for heating homes and chestnut harvesting. The dramatically pruned trees, many of them chestnuts, are part of the restoration. Puncètè, now in ruins, was one hamlet here; it has become an archaeological site.

A foundation, with cantonal support, has restored Curzútt as a destination rather than as a museum. It is part of a larger project with several features that reflect the balance between nature and agriculture here in the past: to restore the forest and grazing lands through careful management by the cantonal forestry department; to create an outdoor laboratory for rare species of plants; to keep motorized vehicles off the mountainside by maintaining old mule paths; to build a water supply from springs that serve restaurants and homes here but that is also a forest fire prevention system. Unemployed workers built the extraordinary long stone walkway that loops around the main village.

Dog friendly hike, but the trail to the bridge is often narrow and busy. Fee for the cable car.

**Notes**
May-November for the entire route. It is feasible in winter, with the risk of snowy, icy sections at the top and on very steep roads. From Curzútt it is possible in winter but weather-dependent and note that the cable car does not stop at mid-stations starting in November, nor is there shuttle bus service from Pairolo, below Curzútt.

# SETTEMAGGIO WINERY

The Marcionetti family business is more than a winery, but wine is its hallmark. Of their 26 hectares, 18 are field crops and grasslands and the remaining 8 are vineyards, most of them on the steep hillsides around the area. This is very much a family handcrafted wines operation. The enthusiasm for quality products and creative marketing solutions make them a standout. The winery is named for the birthday of youngest son Raffaele, who shares the business with his brother Nicola; sister Eliana handles the commercial side and their parents are still actively involved – visitors are likely to be welcomed by their mother, who is very knowledgeable about the wines. This was the first winery to grow PIWI disease-resistant grapes in Ticino, and they remain committed to this approach, which reduces the need for chemical treatments.

 **Tributo:** This is the family's star Merlot, in the sense that it reflects their efforts to achieve the perfect balance between the fruit that is the beauty of Merlot, and the depth that maturing in oak barrels can bring to it. This is their tribute to everyone who has worked over the years to get this balance exactly right.

## ADDRESS

**Settemaggio**
Pedmunt 15
6513 Monte Carasso
Tel: 091 825 6901
Mobile: 079 705 2645
info@settemaggio.ch
settemaggio.ch

## WINERY FEES

No
Regular opening hours, but best to book ahead.

## WHERE ELSE TO FIND THIS CELLAR'S WINES NEARBY

**Grotto Mornera**, 6513 Monte Carasso,
091 825 84 38
grotto@mornera.ch,
**Ristorante Ostello Curzutt**, Via I Fracc 1, 6513 Monte Carasso,
091 835 57 23
curzutt@gastrosos.ch
**Trattoria Er Pipa**, Er Stradun 23, 6513 Monte Carasso,
091 826 45 03
agiuliani@bluewin.ch

# CROGLIO-CASTELROTTO

## ALL THE COLOURS OF THE SOUTH AND GENTLE ANIMALS

SOTTOCENERI - LUGANO

| ▷··· STARTING POINT | ···✗ DESTINATION |
|---|---|
| NOVAGGIO, POSTA BUS STOP | ZÜNDEL AZIENDA AGRICOLA, BERIDE |

| 🗓 SEASON | 🎒 HIKE TYPE |
|---|---|
| **MAY-NOVEMBER** | **MODERATE** 🚶 |

| ⛰ MAP REFERENCE | ⏱ DURATION |
|---|---|
| **SHEET 286T** | **2H 10M** |
| | ↦ LENGTH |
| | **8.5 KM** |
| 🔍 INTERESTING SIGHTS | |
| HOUSE MURAL PAINTINGS IN NOVAGGIO. PANORAMIC VIEWS OF TICINO'S LAKES. HILLTOP VILLAGE OF BEDIGLIORA. | 〰 CLIMB / DESCENT |
| | **315 M / 462 M** |

## ORIZZONTE
ZÜNDEL AZIENDA
AGRICOLA

RED

FULLY RIPE PLUMS AND
BLACK CHERRIES

STARTLING IN ITS FRESHNESS,
PLUM NOTES AGAIN, EXCELLENT
STRUCTURE AND SMOOTH
TANNINS, WELL BALANCED

DRY,
STILL

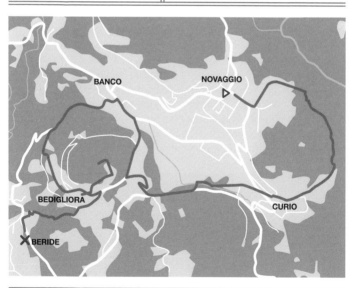

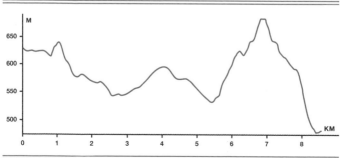

# DESCRIPTION OF THE ROUTE

Novaggio is a busy little town with a regional hospital and streets that go up and down in remarkable ways. From the Novaggio Posta bus stop, take Viale Gisòra away from the center and turn left to begin a loop around the Sciaroni hilltop. Where the road splits, stay left on Via Gána. It shifts from a street to a footpath, always bending right as it makes a large loop around the hilltop, mostly through light woods. It is joined by a path coming in from the left shortly before moving through vineyards along a footpath, Via Sasselli. The trail then rejoins the town, along Piazza Grande. Where it becomes Via Caradora, a footpath, Ra Strecia, strikes off to the left. Cross the Strada Cantonale and take the small road Via Ronchetto, then Via Pre Mulgé. Soon after, cross over the Riale di Molge and continue through the woods along Via Sótt ara Còsta, a farm road.

At a juncture with two roads, take the right-hand option along Viale Pietro Grassi, a road that then makes two hairpin bends as it climbs slightly, followed by a sharp bend to the left as it passes through fields with vineyards below. Take a sharp right onto Via Maria Boschetti Alberti, continuing straight. At an intersection take a left onto Via Cruséta; take the first left onto Strada per Beride. The trail follows this road through the woods, always bending left, and where the Via Néda trail veers off to the left from the road, take it. A lesser footpath veers left, heading towards the village of Bedigliora, joining the Via Bellavista where homes begin to appear. The trail goes through the upper end of the village, then drops to wander through the narrow streets of this typical old Ticinese hilltop village. The trail climbs back up through the village to follow the footpath to the top of the hill, a climb of about 50 meters. The trail retraces the footpath – hikers who don't want to climb

for the view can simply delete this, making the hike about 1 km shorter. The trail rejoins Via Piánca in the town center. Simply follow footpath signs downhill to Beride, which is clearly visible below. This is a mix of woods and farmland, where donkeys, goats, sheep and cows are friendly, curious companions.

The road splits, with Via Néda to the right; continue along the shorter Via Piánca steep footpath into the top end of Beride straight down to the center. Follow the path to the left onto the main road. The winery is on the right after the center and the bus stop.

### Return
There is a bus stop two minutes from the winery in the village center.

### Notes
If there is anything confusing in this part of the world, it is looking at maps and trying to make sense of uphill and downhill – everything twists and turns while changing altitude in surprising ways. Names may mean a hamlet as well as a larger area, so beware of the signs: this is the case with Bedigliora – the final stop at the winery in Beride is part of Bedigloria, for example.

Before setting out to hike, it's worth a stroll around the town of Novaggio to see its many "Murales", wall paintings on houses. The views here are beautiful: Lake Lugano, Ponte Tresa's small lake and the Magliasina valley – Monte Lema is a popular peak for hikers and climbers. Novaggio has a circular 6.5 km, two-hour hike called the Path of Marvels, designed to teach visitors about history and heritage here, with visits to old mills, mines and castles. For anyone staying longer than a day, this is a pleasant additional walk.

Although cars can drive up to Bedigliora, there are not many, and while the edge of the village has some fine new homes, the old village of a chain of linked houses remains intact, so this feels very much like a visit to a town in days of yore. Small rabbit hutches and open air chicken-runs abound; small farming adds to the sense of tranquillity. It's a fine spot for a picnic lunch.

# ZÜNDEL AZIENDA AGRICOLA

Christian Zündel was part of a small wave of Swiss Germans who opted to build wineries in Ticino in the 1980s, often driven by a desire to create very special wines in a relatively untouched environment, frequently working old abandoned vineyards because they were convinced quality wines could be produced here. They had a major impact on winemaking in the region which, as elsewhere in Switzerland, had suffered from over-production and low prices. Several of the newcomers had backgrounds in fields other than winemaking and Zündel was one: he trained at ETZ, the national polytechnic institute in Zurich, as a soils specialist. He was one of Switzerland's earliest vigneron converts to biodynamic farming, and his daughter Myra, who now works with him in the vineyards and the cellar, trained at another pioneering winery, Maison Carrée in Neuchatel.

The emphasis at Zündel's Azienda is on a lack of pretension and mini-malism: great care in the vineyard to make sure the grapes are at their best, and minimal intervention in the cellar, without use of cultured yeasts. The shift has happened gradually, and winelovers who tasted these wines 20 years ago and thought they were very good will be sur-prised at how much better they are.

 **Orizzonte:** Zündel's Merlot blend is in the Mémoire des Vins Suisses to see how well it will age; it is very promising on this score. Only old barrels are used, so there is no hint of oaking, giving a very fresh fruity red wine with good fruit aromas and excellent mouth feel. The only way to achieve this with Merlot is to pick well-tended grapes at optimal ripeness, and then get everything right in the cellar. Merlot grape with 5–10% Cabernet Sauvignon.

## ADDRESS

**Zündel Azienda Agricola**
Beride 25/31
CH-6981 Beride
Tel: 091 608 2440
ufficio@zuendel.ch
zuendel.ch

## WINERY FEES

No
By appointment.

## WHERE ELSE TO FIND THIS CELLAR'S WINES NEARBY

**Bar Saraöö di Giada Manfrini**, 6981 Beride,
091 608 32 26
**La Selvatica**, Maria Boschetti Alberti 9, 6981 Banco,
091 224 53 53
info@laselvatica.ch

# LUGANO

## SOCIABLE WALKING, NATURE AND VINES IN LOVE

SOTTOCENERI -
LUGANO

| ▷⋯ STARTING POINT | ⋯✕ DESTINATION |
|---|---|
| **RIVA CANTONETTO DI GENTILINO BUS STOP, GENTILINO (LUGANO)** | **CANTINA KOPP VON DER CRONE VISINI, BARBENGO** |

| 🗓 SEASON | ▦ HIKE TYPE |
|---|---|
| **YEAR-ROUND** UNLESS RECENT SNOW | **EASY** 🚶 |

| 🗺 MAP REFERENCE | ⏱ DURATION |
|---|---|
| **SHEET 286T** | **2H 15M** |

| | ↦ LENGTH |
|---|---|
| | **7 KM** |

| 🔍 INTERESTING SIGHTS | |
|---|---|
| VIEWS OF LAKE LUGANO. MONTAGNOLA: HERMAN HESSE'S HOUSE, CASA CAMUZZI. | 〰 CLIMB / DESCENT |
| | **421 M / 322 M** |

MERLOT (BLEND)

# BALIN
## CANTINA KOPP VON DER CRONE VISINI

RED

INTENSE AND DEEPLY PLEASING: PLUMS, BLACK CHERRIES, BLACKCURRANTS, HINTS OF TOASTING AND LICORICE

VELVETY: DARK CHOCOLATE, TOASTED ALMONDS, BLACK-CURRANT SWEETS, VERY LONG FINISH

DRY, STILL

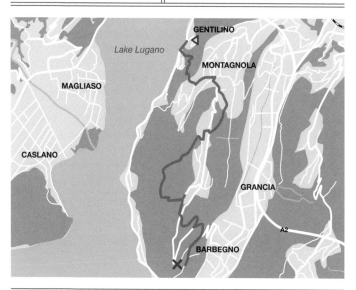

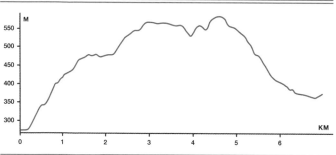

# DESCRIPTION OF THE ROUTE

From the bus stop on the lakefront at Cantonetto di Gentilino, walk a few meters before turning left and uphill onto the Val d'Orino marked footpath. It turns right, running parallel to the lake; continue straight until just before Selva Piana, when the path jogs left then right into the village. The footpath turns left; where the paved street begins, turn right onto a short footpath that leads to Via Marianda; turn left. Continue a short distance and where the road splits, take the right fork: Via Credee, which leads into the center of Montagnola, which is where writer Hermann Hesse spent the early years of his life (it's a short detour to the house/museum). At the T-junction, turn right and look for signs for the Charme de la Collina d'Oro hiking trail. Stay on this street, Via H. Hesse, until it ends and becomes a footpath; continue straight, mainly through woods, following signs for Bigogno. The trail climbs slightly through airy open woods.

Once in the long, strung-out village, cross the Collina d'Oro road to Via Cappelletta and turn left and walk until the road splits: take a sharp right and follow the street as it bends right and becomes a footpath. The next part of the trail is through the woods, circling Monte Croce, at one point skirting an open field which is to the left. At another point, after bending left, there are vineyards on the right. At the entrance to a small village the trail takes a very sharp right and begins to head downhill, passing the Collina d'Oro resort (on the right) and crossing over the Roncone road. The trail then zigzags down through woodland and vineyards, joining the Via Agra briefly at the bottom of a vineyard. Stay on the road after it takes a sharp right, and enter the narrow street of the old town of Barbengo (Via alla Chiesa). Follow signs for the winery, staying on the street: at the cemetery the road splits. Take the right-hand road and the winery is just after the cemetery.

**Return**
Allow at least 20 minutes to get to the bus stop.

**Notes**
This is an excellent family walk. It follows, for much of the way, a well-known Colina d'Oro route from Montagnola to Carona. The trail here starts on the western side of Lake Lugano, to take advantage of the quietly beautiful shoreline before climbing up to the top of the hill, which is a ridge above the two arms of Lake Lugano with several hiking trails and sports centres. It is very popular – expect to see dogs and families, athletes and people out for a breath of fresh air. The trail stops at the winery; for those looking for a more demanding outing, allow another 2 hours to walk to Carona along the marked Charme de la Colina d'Oro trail.

# CANTINA KOPP VON DER CRONE VISINI

This is a remarkable winery, on several levels. It was created in 2006 by merging two wineries that had worked closely together for four years. Their 7 hectares of vineyard are spread over three regions in Ticino: Mendrisiotto, Lugano and Bellinzona, a daunting challenge in terms of distances from the winery in Barbengo, but also for managing very different soil types and growing conditions. Anna Barbara von der Crone, who grew up in Zurich, and Paolo Visini, have created a vision of what excellent wines should be: combine the earthiness and beauty of Ticino with an understanding of what knowledgeable urban consumers want. They grow traditional grapes – Merlot is 70% – and disease-resistant and other specialty grapes, working with "alternative pesticides" but using no insecticides or herbicides, a challenge given the humid conditions here. The third winery name is from Anna Barbara's husband, Ueli Kopp, with whom in 1994 she founded one of the two wineries that later merged, and who died when their four children were small.

 **Balin:** This wine has for years won awards and praise, as a wine with great depth, balance – harmonious. This signature wine in some ways makes it easy to overlook the fact that the creative, innovative duo at work here have built an extraordinary, varied wine list, working with grapes from several areas in Ticino. Merlot grape, about 6% other (Arinarnoa, 1% Cabernet Sauvignon).

## ADDRESS

**Kopp von der Crone Visini**
Via Noga 2
CH-6917 Barbengo
Tel: 091 682 96 16
info@cantinabarbengo.ch
cantinabarbengo.ch

## WINERY FEES

CHF 30 for cellar tour and tasting session. Reservation required.

## WHERE ELSE TO FIND THIS CELLAR'S WINES NEARBY

**Grotto dell'Ortiga**, Str. Regina 35, 6928 Manno,
091 605 16 13
ortiga@bluewin.ch
**Bottegone del Vino**, Via Magatti 3, 6900 Lugano,
091 922 76 89
bottegonelugano@gmail.com

# MORCOTE

## PEAK TO LAKE'S-END CASTLE BEAUTY

SOTTOCENERI - LUGANO

| ▷··· STARTING POINT | ···✕ DESTINATION |
|---|---|
| **PARADISO (NEAR LUGANO) FUNICULAR STATION** | **TENUTA CASTELLO DI MORCOTE, VICO MORCOTE** |

| 📅 SEASON | 🗺 HIKE TYPE |
|---|---|
| **YEAR-ROUND,** WEATHER PERMITTING | **MODERATE /DIFFICULT**   |

| 🗺 MAP REFERENCE | ⏲ DURATION |
|---|---|
| **SHEET 286T** | **3H 30M** |

| | ↦ LENGTH |
|---|---|
| | **11.8 KM** |

| 🔍 INTERESTING SIGHTS | 〰 CLIMB / DESCENT |
|---|---|
| PARCO SAN GRATO BOTANICAL GARDENS. ALPE VICANIA'S PASTURES. HISTORICAL VINEYARDS AND WINERY CASTLE. | **421 M / 867 M** |

MERLOT 90%, CABERNET FRANC 10%

# CASTELLO DI MORCOTE
TENUTA CASTELLO DI MORCOTE

 RED

 BLACKBERRIES, AROMATIC, SLIGHTLY SMOKY

 FULL, RICH, WELL STRUCTURED, EXCEPTIONALLY ELEGANT

 DRY, STILL, OAKED ONE YEAR IN BARRELS

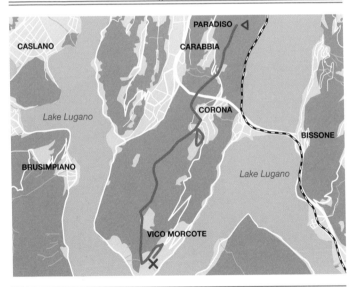

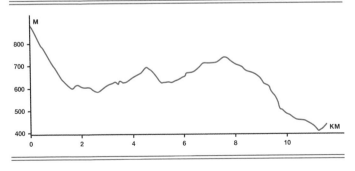

# DESCRIPTION OF THE ROUTE

The funicular up to Monte San Salvatore from the center of Paradiso is the way to get to the top, as the hike up is very steep, mostly wooded and mainly of interest to fitness buffs. Once at the often-busy top, where day-tripper crowds are looking at the view or waiting in line for the restaurant, look carefully at the hiking signposts. Avoid the red and white tough-hike diamond signs that take you back down to Paradiso. Walk around the side of the restaurant until you see the yellow hiking trail signs. This is where you begin heading down dozens and dozens of log stairs, through peaceful woods with occasional views over to the west side of the lake and Italy.

The downhill wooded walk is easy and pleasant, coming out suddenly into the hamlet of Ciona and, soon after, the village of Carona. The architecture and colours are old Italian. Carona, accessible by the

Lugano-Vico Morcote road and Melide, can get busy with tourists. It is famous as a longtime home to architects and craftsmen, and its narrow streets and homes with frescoes are worth a wander. Follow signs for the San Grato botanical gardens, a haven of rhododendrons, azaleas and much more, with six trails inside the 200,000m² park. The village is also home to the Madonna d'Ongero sanctuary with baroque frescoes and the 13th century Torello Monastery, a detour from the trail.

Coming out of Carona, it is easy to be confused because all trails seem marked to lead to Vico Morcote. As a general rule, if you're not using the GPX file, follow the sign for the footpath with the shortest hiking time. Between Carona and the Alpe Vicania restaurant, you spend an hour in an airy, open forest rich in wildlife – mostly but not always hidden.

The trail to the winery from the restaurant follows the daunting steps of the public trail straight downhill from the western side of the restaurant. The path runs along the walls of the 15th century castle of Vico

Morcote, which remains at the center of the vineyard and gives its name to the winery. Once close to the church of Santa Maria del Sasso in Morcote there is a path on the left leading to the entrance of the winery.

Vico Morcote, uphill from the town of Morcote, is a well-preserved typical Ticino hillside village of narrow streets, porticos and fine old homes, worth exploring.

**Return**
Bus service from Vico Morcote center to Morcote and Melide, train connection to Lugano.

**Notes**
Alpe Vicania is often described as pastures with horses roaming freely, but it is also part of a very large organic farming and research project that includes the Tenuta Castello di Morcote organic winery. The view from the winery's vineyards is spectacular, even by Ticino mountain and lake views standards.

Forewarned if you don't like stairs – there are an impressive number at the outset and the finish.

# TENUTA CASTELLO DI MORCOTE

Gaby Gianini, an art historian turned family wine boss, transformed the *tenuta* in a dozen years into a forward-looking organic winery. The 12 hectares of vineyard are part of the larger 150 hectares of the whole farm and research area reserve. The star wine here is the Castello di Morcote Riserva, 90% Merlot and 10% Cabernet Franc, but the other wines also showcase what granite and porphyry (coarse-grained crystals rock) soils, and the special winds that sweep over this tip of the promontory, can give to wines.

 **Castello di Morcote:** a quality classic Merlot from the region.

## ADDRESS

**Tenuta Castello di Morcote**
Strada al Castel 28
6921 Vico Morcote
Tel: 091 996 1230
info@castellodimorcote.ch
castellodimorcote.ch

## WINERY FEES

Visits by appointment; ask about fees.

## WHERE ELSE TO FIND THIS CELLAR'S WINES NEARBY

**Ristorante Vicania**, 6921 Vico Morcote,
091 980 24 14
info@ristorantevicania.ch

# CAPOLAGO

## THE ITALIAN CORNER OF TICINO
## VIA ARCHAEOLOGY AND ARCHITECTURE

SOTTOCENERI - MENDRISIO

|  STARTING POINT |  DESTINATION |
|---|---|
| **BESAZIO CRUSAGH BUS STOP** (15 MINUTES BY BUS FROM THE MENDRISIO TRAIN STATION) | **CASTELLO DI CANTONE, CAPOLAGO** |

|  SEASON | HIKE TYPE |
|---|---|
| **YEAR-ROUND** | **MODERATE /DIFFICULT**   |

| MAP REFERENCE | DURATION |
|---|---|
| **SHEET 286T** | **2H 30M** |
| | LENGTH |
| | **8.7 KM** |

**INTERESTING SIGHTS**

RUINS AT RUDERI DEL CASTELLO.
VIEWS OF MONTE GENEROSO.
MONTE SAN GIORGIO FOSSILS MUSEUM.
OLDEST CHRISTIAN STONE MONUMENT IN
SWITZERLAND.

**CLIMB / DESCENT**

**317 M / 542 M**

# MERLOT RISERVA
## CASTELLO DI CANTONE

RED

COMPLEX: RIPE BLACK AND
SMALL RED BERRIES,
VANILLA, HINTS OF TOBACCO
AND SWEET SPICES

RICH, DEEP, ELEGANT,
TASTES OF VERY RIPE BERRIES,
SILKY TANNINS THAT NEED TIME
TO SETTLE

DRY,
STILL

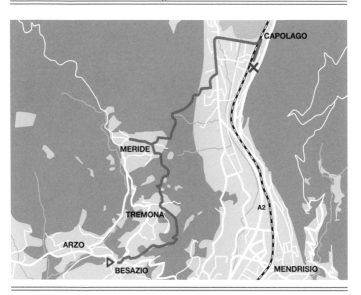

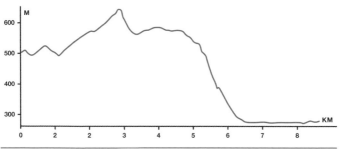

# DESCRIPTION OF THE ROUTE

From the bus stop in Besazio, walk back downhill a few meters and turn left onto Via Sant' Antonino. Turn right very soon after, just below the church, following the footpath signs downhill into and through the village – left at Ferdinando Bustelli, left again at Via alla Cava and then stay on this as it becomes a footpath uphill and out of town. This is a very pretty stone and dirt walk between vineyards that winds around the hillside; stay on the trail (Via Barozzo) with signs pointing to Tremona. Where the trail splits, take the left, uphill path, which is the continuation of Via Barozzo and carry on until Tremona. The path ends at a T-junction with Via Antonio Rinaldi. Turn right and at the next intersection take the second street: go straight and uphill along Via al Castello but when this street turns right, carry on straight, following signs for the Ruderi del Castello archaeological ruins, which are well worth the 20-step detour to the right. They are hidden from the trail. At the exit from the ruins, rejoin the trail and from here to Meride simply follow

the yellow trail arrows through the wooded hillside, with a somewhat steep descent just before reaching the town.

The trail here takes a short detour to the left to walk through the town with its fine old homes, narrow streets and a museum on the right which was designed by Ticino's world-class architect Mario Botta. Monte San Giorgio is famous as a repository for ancient fossils and the museum displays a fine collection of these. Retrace steps through the village to the small stone San Antonio shrine where the marked trail continues left along the street A Sant' Antonio. Shortly after the street ends and a dirt trail begins, the trail splits: take the right-hand option. When the trail splits again, just as it bends to the left, be sure to stay on the left. Simply follow the trail signs from here to the town of Riva San Vitale, crossing over a small stream at one point and crossing another trail (carry on straight). The trail climbs down some 200 meters and twists and turns to accommodate the terrain, but it is essentially a straight line to the town.

The path turns into a street that bends right quite soon, with vineyards on the right; stay on the street, Via alle Pianche, as it bends left to head into the town center, then right after the cemetery. At the T-junction with Via Giuseppe Motta turn left. Stay on this street as it becomes Via Settala;

the beautiful Battistero di Riva San Vitale is on the right after the Oratoria – follow signs to visit. Via Settala leads into Piazza Grande, veering right. Continue until Via dell'Indipendenza; turn right and follow this lakeside road straight, across the Laveggio River; the street changes name. Shortly before the railway tracks and highway above the town, this street turns right and here, look for a narrow path, just after Via Lüera to the left. Take this footpath to cross rails and highway and a local road. It climbs up to Capolago, a long strip of a village that is also home to the start of Switzerland's oldest operating rack steam train, up to Monte Generoso. Take Via Municipio, which runs parallel to the main train line, almost to the end of the street. The winery is on the left.

## Return
Five minutes by foot to the Capolago train station.

## Notes
This is a young and small operation and it can be difficult to reach this busy couple, but they are among the hottest young winemakers in Switzerland, and tasting their wines is an eye-opener. Merlot is by far the dominant grape in Ticino and it is made in different styles, but the approach here is different, strongly influenced by Italian winemaking.

# CASTELLO DI CANTONE

Think Italy, when in Mendrisio, which is part of Switzerland but with centuries of long, strong ties to Italy. The border is just three fields away from the start of this trail and Milan is visible from the archaeological ruins just after Tremona. Viviana Pasta and Dario Pistarà met while oenology students at the University of Milan. He then went to work for top wineries in Italy while she continued her studies in

Bordeaux, with training in Australia. They married and initially rented vines planted in the 1990s from carefully selected French stock. From the beginning, they had dreams of making great Merlots that would age beautifully for an international market. Their first wine came out in 2016. The grapes are mainly grown in Rancate, vines that are part of the Monte San Giorgio UNESCO World Heritage Site, an area long known to be good for viticulture partly because temperatures are modified by the mountain and Lake Lugano. They've purchased more vines and today produce from 15 hectares. The wine is made in an old cellar in nearby Capolago but the couple are planning a new winery. Capolago is the departure point for the rack train up to Monte Generoso, Ticino's highest mountain, whose other side is in Italy with Lake Como at the bottom.

 **Castello di Cantone Merlot Riserva:** This pair of young winemakers have given themselves the task of making great Merlot wines that will age well, in the manner of some of the best Italian and French wines. They've already achieved this with two "extreme dried" wines, a Merlot, Cru°dei°Folli and Ungulus, a Cabernet Franc. These are made only in vintages that allow the quality they seek. They are matured in new oak for two years, then aged in bottles for two years before they are released. It's clear that these wines need time and they can seem almost too big for their boots when young, but they can still be appreciated in their early years. The Castello di Cantone Merlot Riserva grapes are picked relatively late, fully ripe, and then they are dried for three weeks before they are pressed in the *appassimento* style of Valpolicella grapes in Italy. The wine is made very slowly in concrete tanks and it then matures in oak barrels for 14–18 months.

## ADDRESS

**Castello di Cantone**
Via Municipio 6
6825 Capolago
Tel: 091 630 6000
castellodicantone.ch

## WINERY FEES

No. By appointment.

## WHERE ELSE TO FIND THIS CELLAR'S WINES NEARBY

**Porto Pojana Ristorante Terminus**, Via Poiana 53, 6826 Riva San Vitale, 091 630 63 70
ristorante@portopojana.ch

# TOP 5

## MY 5 FAVOURITE WINERIES

**CAVES FRÈRES DUTRUY** – Founex

**DOMAINE LE PETIT CHÂTEAU** – Môtier

**RUTISHAUSER WEINGUT AM STEINIG TISCH** – St. Gallen-Thal

**CASTELLO DI MORCOTE** – Vico di Morcote

**MONT D'OR** – Sion

## MY 5 FAVOURITE HIKES

**MAIENFELD** – Graubünden

**MONTE CARASSO** – Ticino

**RARON** – Valais

**SAINT-PIERRE-DE-CLAGES** – Valais

**ARAN VILLETTE** – Vaud (especially combined with Cully)

# IN NUMBERS

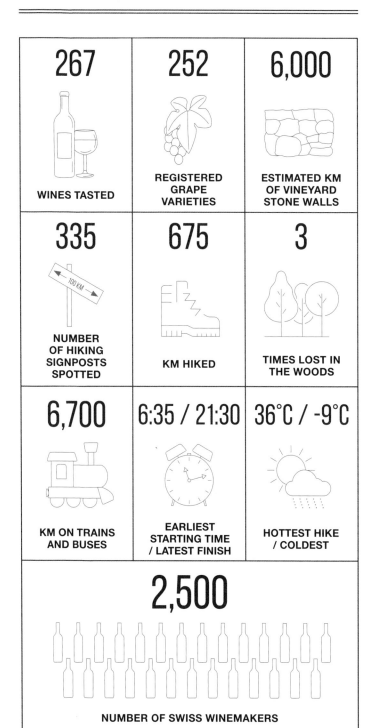

| 267 | 252 | 6,000 |
|:---:|:---:|:---:|
| WINES TASTED | REGISTERED GRAPE VARIETIES | ESTIMATED KM OF VINEYARD STONE WALLS |

| 335 | 675 | 3 |
|:---:|:---:|:---:|
| NUMBER OF HIKING SIGNPOSTS SPOTTED | KM HIKED | TIMES LOST IN THE WOODS |

| 6,700 | 6:35 / 21:30 | 36°C / -9°C |
|:---:|:---:|:---:|
| KM ON TRAINS AND BUSES | EARLIEST STARTING TIME / LATEST FINISH | HOTTEST HIKE / COLDEST |

## 2,500

NUMBER OF SWISS WINEMAKERS

# ACKNOWLEDGEMENTS

Two groups of very generous people get a big thumbs up from me. One is Switzerland's artisanal vignerons who routinely and enthusiastically help me understand their work and their wines. My biggest regret is that I couldn't fit all of them into this book.

The other is all the volunteers who maintain and mark the extraordinary 66,000 km of hiking trails in Switzerland that make this country a precious jewel for anyone who likes to walk.

Thanks also go to the many wine bodies that have provided up-to-date and accurate information for the book, from the Swiss Federal Agriculture office to Swiss Wine, the promotional organization, and marketing organizations for each of the six official wine regions. Two groups of which I am proud to be an invited member have helped bring me to this point in my wine knowledge: the Mémoire des Vins Suisses and the international Circle of Wine Writers; thank you to fellow members who continue to teach me so much.

A very treasured group is those friends who are happy to share a glass of wine or two, often wines that are new to them. David and Evelyn, thank you for the beautiful meals with our wines. Liam and Jess, thank you for the perspective of the next generation. To Michael Ribordy, who replaced both of my knees in 2016 and then said "walk at least an hour a day for the rest of your life", and therapist Didier Collard who nursed along my tendonitis in a heel while doing this book, thank you for keeping me on my feet. And a bow to the past, to my mother who loved to walk and set an example well into her nineties and her father, also a walker until he died at 91, who taught her and then me, that you can walk your way through sorrow to joy, or just walk because it's a great way to keep learning about the world.

**Wine Hiking Switzerland**
Explore the Landscape of Swiss Wines
Ellen Wallace

Text: Ellen Wallace
Photography: Ellen Wallace
Typsetting and layout: Daniel Malak and Ajša Zdravković
Editors: Shelby Stuart, Jonas Gut, Aude Pidoux
Proofreader: Karin Waldhauser

ISBN: 978-3-907293-86-7

First Edition: September 2022
Deposit copy in Switzerland: September 2022
Printed in Czech Republic

© 2022 HELVETIQ (Helvetiq Sàrl)
Av. des Acacias 7
CH-1006 Lausanne, Switzerland

Excessive drinking may damage your health, drink with moderation.
Don't drink and drive.

MIX
Paper from
responsible sources
FSC® C014138

www.helvetiq.com